The Return of Radicalis

Recasting Marxism

Boris Kagarlitsky

New Realism, New Barbarism

The Twilight of Globalization

The Return of Radicalism
Reshaping the Left Institutions

Boris Kagarlitsky

Translated by Renfrey Clarke

Pluto **AP** Press

LONDON • STERLING, VIRGINIA

First published 2000 by Pluto Press
345 Archway Road, London N6 5AA
and 22883 Quicksilver Drive,
Sterling, VA 21066–2012, USA

British Library Cataloguing in Publication Data
A catalogue record for this book is available from
the British Library

ISBN 0 7453 1596 8 hbk

Library of Congress Cataloging in Publication Data
Kagarlitsky, Boris, 1958–
    The return of radicalism : reshaping the left institutions / Boris
    Kagarlitsky.
        p. cm.— (Recasting Marxism)
    Includes bibliographical references and index.
    ISBN 0–7453–1596–8
        1. Socialism. 2. Radicalism. I. Title. II. Series.

HX44.5.K36 2000
335.4—dc21   99–046658

Designed and produced for Pluto Press by
Chase Production Services, Chadlington, OX7 3LN
Typeset from disk by Stanford DTP Services, Northampton
Printed in the European Union by TJ International, Padstow

Contents

Preface

This is the concluding book of *Recasting Marxism* and it is probably less theoretical then the other two. In the first book I try to prove that Marxism is not only relevant but also needs de-revision. The second book is about institutions and strategies. Finally, in this book I discuss the political forces that can bring about change.

I start with the crisis of the trade unions and with attempts to revive them. The story of the death of trade unionism was heavily exaggerated. It is noteworthy that the decline of the trade unions in the countries of the 'centre' is being accompanied by their rapid growth on the 'periphery', above all in the new industrial countries. However, it does not follow from this that the traditional forms of trade union action are now adequate even in the Third World or in Eastern Europe. The unions have a role to play. We need them in the era of globalization even more than before. To cope with their new role the unions must change. In place of vertical, 'monolithic' structures, new 'networks', based on coordination via horizontal links, are beginning to be constructed. But the most important change that is needed in order to revive unionism is ideological. In the era of globalization the unions can be successful only if they understand their potential as a force of change, as an anti-capitalist, anti-systemic movement.

The second chapter of the book is called 'Beyond Identities', and, as one can easily guess, it is devoted to a critique of the post-modernist left. I know that a lot of people in the West will see my approach as controversial, but I have to say what I think. Contrary to some Western interpretations, the experience of Eastern Europe and of the Third World shows the vital need for a universalist left as the *only real alternative* to diverse forms of barbarism. The critique of feminism and of identity politics does not mean, of course, that earlier forms of the left movement were that good. It could be said that the postmodernists are right in their criticism of many aspects of the ideology and actions of the 'old left', just as the traditional left is correct in its criticism of postmodernist radicalism. The task is to find new political means for realizing traditional goals.

The final chapter, 'The Third Left or the Third Socialism', examines the state of the contemporary left, with a discussion of the 'third left' (Andersson)[1] and the 'third socialism' (Amin),[2] and also of the experience of such left parties and movements of the 'new wave' as the German Party of Democratic Socialism, the Workers' Party in Brazil, and the Zapatistas. Not only the successes of these formations, but also their problems and failures provide extremely important material for developing the strategy of the left in new conditions. The dissimilarities between these parties and movements and the impossibility of a mechanical transfer of experience between them constitute an important *general* trait of the 'new wave' leftists.

The left is now entering a new stage in its history and we are taking just the first steps into the unknown. It is important to make these steps with our eyes and hearts open, with political courage and analytical sharpness. We must keep discussing socialist theory – that is why I wrote this book – but we must also act.

This book is about organizations and people in struggle. I hope that it will help people in struggle.

Introduction: Pride and Protest

The twentieth century has unquestionably been the epoch of the struggle between capitalism and the 'communist system'. Capitalism won this struggle. Nevertheless, the final years of the twentieth century have not been a time of triumph. On the contrary, the victory of the West over the Soviet Union, the transformation of the former super-power into a semi-colonial periphery, and the global revenge exacted by capital in its struggle against labour have revealed all the contradictions of the capitalist system on an unprecedented scale. To say the least, capitalism is not entering the new century in a particularly good state. The system is simply incapable of functioning normally on the basis of its own logic. But however deep the crisis of capitalism, the crisis of the left movement is even deeper. Demoralization and conscious treachery, the opening of a broad gulf between the 'left' political class and the workers, a lack of new ideas and the bureaucratic degeneration of the old organizations – these are merely a few of the visible symptoms of this crisis.

The international communist movement disappeared together with the Soviet Union. Social democratic parties originally expected to strengthen their positions with the collapse of communism. In reality they also entered a long period of crisis in the 1990s. By the end of the decade they had recovered in electoral terms but not politically. Ironically, it was in Eastern Europe where electoral left made the fastest comeback. This was not followed by any change in social policies or economic priorities of the state. The people were frustrated and quite soon social democratic parties in the East were voted out of office.

The impotence and irresponsibility of the left are all the more striking when viewed against the background of capitalism's growing systemic crisis. In 1998 and 1999 leftists or centre-leftists were in power in all the main countries of Europe, from Britain to Russia, from Italy to Sweden. In Britain and Italy 'left-wing' governments began immediately to pursue openly right-wing policies. In France and Russia left-wing prime ministers, coexisting with right-wing presidents, tried to pursue a compromise course, avoiding the extremes of neo-liberalism but

1

at the same time failing to make a radical break with the past. The government of Evgeny Primalov in Russia was forced to resign after eight successful months when its popularity in the opinion polls had reached record levels. The government surrendered power without much struggle. But however much we might criticize the weakness of the 'centre-left', it is clear that it is not these people who have been the main problem. Th greatest problem has been the powerlessness of the radical forces, which are incapable of placing the centre-left under noticeable pressure. Every 'left' government today encounters very strong pressure from the right – from the bourgeoisie, from international financial institutions and from corrupt bureaucrats. Only rarely does it come under pressure from the left. Even where the mass movement makes its presence felt, the left parties, with few exceptions, are incapable of providing the movement with strategic perspectives, or of becoming its political expression.

For many observers in the early 1990s the Green parties looked much more promising than the 'old' left. In Nordic countries left-wing socialist forces competing with social democrats endorsed ecological issues and transformed themselves into 'red-green' formations. Robin Blackburn, the editor of *New Left Review* saw in these movements a potential for 'transforming the historic programmes of the Left'. According to Blackburn, 'these "New Left" formations typically define themselves in relation to regional, continental and global issues rather than mainly to the sphere of national political life: ecology, migrant labour, anti-racism and anti-militarism being key concerns'. Their programmes 'do not yet comprise a fully comprehensive and coherent package that could replace the logic of capitalism. But there are here a variety of models, measures and movements from which an effective programme promises to develop.'[1] In reality the innovative potential of these parties and movements turned out to be very limited. At the same time, the leading circles of the 'New Left' formations proved to be quite complaisant to political corruption. The Green parties were gradually losing their identity as a radical force without acquiring a real reformist culture. Intellectuals were no better than the politicians. Postmodernist fashion freed the intellectuals from their traditional ethics. Instead of criticizing reality they tried to adjust to it.

Former radical intellectuals started speaking enthusiastically about 'the New Times' bringing about dramatic technological and social change. They rushed to proclaim that 'the political party as we have known it is an anachronism', that we 'need to move beyond the idea of socialism as the unifying apex for left politics', or even 'beyond left and right' towards 'participatory radicalism'.[2] All this was not accompanied by even a minimal analysis of the technological and social transformation which was really happening. Instead, most of the propaganda myths of the neo-liberals were uncritically accepted.

The crisis of the left movement is usually seen as having three causes: the disintegration of the 'communist bloc'; globalization; and the technological revolution. It is true that these developments have made it impossible for the left to remain as it was. But in the new conditions, the need for a radical anti-capitalist alternative has become greater, not less.

The technological revolution has not led to the supplanting of the old economic and social order by the virtual economy or the network society. All that has happened is that new economic and social structures have been superimposed on the old, complicating all the processes involved and making them harder to manage. However often the disappearance of the peasantry has been predicted, the peasantry still exists. With the demographic explosion, it is even growing. While we are promised that industrial workers will disappear 'as a class', on the scale of the planet as a whole their numbers are increasing. Meanwhile, huge numbers of people who are needed neither in the cities nor in the countryside are gathering on the margins (in both the figurative and literal senses), trying to make a living from the most primitive, unskilled types of work. These people, many millions of them, not only inhabit a world totally unconnnected to the computer or the factory work-bench, but are also quite unable to return to the patriarchal world of the past. They are part of a growing army of economic 'informals', an army that is constantly gaining new battalions, from post-Soviet 'shuttle traders' to Latin American and Arab street vendors. They represent a mass of workers who are perfectly competitive, since their labour power costs almost nothing. Whatever the improvements to the automobile, it cannot drive the rickshaw off the streets of Asian cities. For cheapness, the most advanced agro-technologies cannot compare with Chinese peasants, growing rice in their fields using the same methods as in the time of Confucius.

People sitting at computers doing clean jobs, perhaps not even leaving their homes while they immerse themselves in the Internet, at times simply refuse to notice this mass of 'unmodernized' human beings. One section of the techno-elite is inclined to ignore their existence altogether, while another, more humane section, is convinced that everything is just a matter of time. The techno-elite hopes that in the near future, as resources increase, technology will make it possible to find answers to all the accumulated problems, resolve all the contradictions and simply perform an upgrade on all the people who have remained 'outside the bounds of progress'. Meanwhile, left-wing politicians, sitting in parliaments and speaking at conferences, are less and less likely to encounter these incomprehensible beings from the world of the 'unmodernized'. The politicians do not understand this world, and do not notice it, in exactly the same way as in ancient civilizations people were unwilling to notice and understand the barbarians. And the arrogant postmodernist intellectuals don't want to recognize that there is a growing number of people who will never swallow their theories.

The Industrial Revolution developed according to the 'pyramid principle'. Development began on a broad basis, with virtually the whole society drawn into the process. But by no means everyone had to change his or her way of life radically in order to participate. Each new technological 'floor' was smaller and narrower than the preceding one, but at the same time rested on the preceding one, answered its requirements and served as its 'peak'. The processes occurring on the upper floors had a direct impact on those further down. This was not always pleasant for the inhabitants of the lower floors; they were forced at times to raise themselves up against their will. Several generations were needed for technological modernization to be organically assimilated. A peasant became an industrial worker, while his or her descendants gained an education and became engineers, representatives of the new middle class, and finally came to make up the backbone of today's technological elite. Economic progress was perceived as a natural precondition for social progress, and everyday experience confirmed this. The labour movement rested on a natural social dynamic: upward mobility for the representatives of the 'lower classes' increased simultaneously with the development of industry.

The self-confident evolutionary optimism of social democracy was based on historical experience. Constant attempts were made to leap across 'intermediate stages', but these attempts invariably failed. The price of 'acceleration' became steadily higher. The Soviet Union paid for it with decades of emotional and social stress, not to speak of the cost in lives. The countries of the Third World simply failed to cope. The Arab-Israeli wars of 1967 and 1973 showed that it was possible to teach Egyptian *fellahin* to use anti-aircraft rocket complexes, but that it was far more difficult to teach them to win a war using these weapons. Transmitting technical knowledge was relatively easy, but this knowledge was useless without the experience and culture that corresponded to it.

By the late twentieth century the Industrial Revolution had exhausted itself, and capitalism made a new technological break-through that showed how naive the technological optimism of the preceding generations had been. In the sphere of technology, the 'skyscraper principle' began to triumph. Instead of a slow and painful dragging of society into a new way of life for which society at times did not feel any particularly need, preference was now given to a rapid movement 'onward and upward'.

The skyscraper of technological revolution is growing before our eyes. While particular floors are still being settled into, new ones are already being built. The stages of this revolution are self-sufficient. What is demanded of us is that we should continually raise ourselves upward in order not to fall behind. People, like computers, are in need of constant upgrades.

This process, however, is occurring in a relatively confined field. Of 34 million users of the Internet in 1996, two-thirds were in the US. On the scale of humanity as a whole this is infinitesimal, and even in the country that is the leader of the world computer revolution it represents a minority. In Russia the number of people who have computers is almost thirty times fewer than in America and, although this number is growing, the American level will not be reached in the next decade. This means that it will never be reached, since in ten years' time new floors of the technological skyscraper will have been built in the countries of the 'centre'. The capacity of the average computer in Russia, however, is much the same as in America. In other words, the process of improving already existing equipment is occurring far more rapidly than its spread to new population groups. Ten years ago Soviet economists were justly counterposing the 'extensive' growth of industry in the USSR to the 'intensive' model in the West, where production was growing not because new factories were being built, but because new technologies were being introduced. Now the intensive model is giving birth to insoluble contradictions of its own.

The high growth rates of new technologies are often cited as confirming the thesis that paradisiacal levels of consumption will soon become accessible to all. To those who take this approach, the crisis and stagnation in the 'traditional sector' appears almost to confirm the belief that universal happiness is in sight. Renovated by network structures and information technologies, capitalism will become, if not completely inoffensive, then at least perfectly acceptable as a way of life. In reality, high growth rates are a feature of any new technology in its initial stages. Here, it is easier to set something going than to continue to make progress. It was easier to create the Internet than it has been to maintain order in it. The present rapid spread of the network merely signifies that it is still at the stage of becoming established. The more massive the scale of a phenomenon, the more difficult it is to maintain growth. But the skyscraper requires movement 'upward' even when spreading 'sideways' is impossible. While some people are making their tenth upgrade, others are still without a computer at all. Nor are they likely to acquire one.

The point is not simply that most people do not have the money for a computer. Many do not feel they need one either. It is characteristic of technocrats to complain constantly that people do not behave as they are supposed to. Instead of joining in the race, people would rather take a breather. In their arrogance, the technological elite fail to notice that society is growing tired of the pace of change that is being imposed on it, that the demand for new technologies is falling. No one is asking 'Why?' One has the impression that new technologies are now being created with the sole aim of providing a springboard for the development of new, even more modern technologies. Society's resistance is proving to be unconscious and mainly passive. Although there are growing numbers of reactionaries and fundamentalists of all conceivable types, people who basically loathe the very idea of progress, most people are far more peaceably inclined. They are not against upgrading in principle; they have simply stopped feeling that they need it themselves.

The people who inhabit the 'middle floors' of the skyscraper have withdrawn into themselves. They perceive what is coming from above not as indispensable help, but as aggressive pressure. The 'middle floors' are a dull world of traditional industrial technologies, of a habitual urban way of life. The techno-elite, in their arrogance, perceive all this as part of the vanishing past and therefore are unable and unwilling to offer anything to the inhabitants of the 'middle floors'. But the techno-elite cannot do without these people. Someone has to assemble computers (often in grimy sheds somewhere near the northern border of Mexico or on the outskirts of Moscow). Someone has to use them (apart, of course, from the programmers themselves). Most importantly, people have to come to the 'upper floors' from somewhere.

If we are living on the upper floors, life is fascinating and unpredictable. Round about us something is always being built, some structure or other is being moved somewhere, something is being tested out. But if we look down, we have the sense that nothing is happening there, and when young people break out of this dull routine, they do not want to look back. Here, though, is the problem: with every year, the new recruits to the technological revolution are fewer and fewer. In the US and Canada there is a shortage of highly skilled workers. At the same time, millions of educated people in other countries cannot find work. What is this – the first stage in the formation of a global labour market? No, it is simply a new stage in the violence wrought by capitalism against the individual, since people are not a resource that can simply be loaded onto aircraft and transported from place to place. They love their homes, their languages, their countries. Why should people have to move to where there is work? Why cannot the work be moved to where there are people?

At the same time as there are personnel shortages at one pole, at the other there is chronic unemployment. Unskilled workers are usually unable to master a new profession, and in the meantime, there are no jobs for them. The technological elite will not devote itself to perfecting technologies that are consciously oriented to the epoch before the last. The inhabitants of the 'upper floors' can replenish their ranks only with people from the 'middle floors'. There, however, the potential is almost exhausted. The people who are relatively young and dynamic have already made their way up into the elite. And what about the dwellers on the 'lower floors', and the people outside the gates of the 'building'? For them, the skyscraper is too high. Breaking through from the lower floors straight to the top is simply impossible. The only prospects are of making it to the 'middle floors'. But at this level there is no demand for new people. Nor are there any particular incentives to rise to the 'middle floors'; here there is only stagnation and dullness.

Success, mobility and the ability to make one's own choices are becoming privileges of the inhabitants of the 'top floor'. Life on the bottom floors is no longer either interesting, or capable of providing people with self-respect. There is no ardour, nothing to strive for. The technological elite is not in the least hostile to everyone else. It is criminally indifferent to them. But this, in the final analysis, is a crucial weakness. Lacking a broad base, the process begins to falter.

Rapid changes cannot be maintained without let-up. Techno-logical revolution, like political revolution, cannot be permanent; pauses are essential if progress is to be made. In order to haul people up onto a new technological level, it is not enough to present new inventions and to wait for the suspicious masses to grow used to them. Nor, in a stratified society, can any help be expected from the 'invisible hand of the market', with which liberal economists love to frighten us. The movement has to begin from above, and one's eyes have to be fixed not on the elite, but on the bottom floors. To raise people up is a daunting proposition, and the more the technological elite in its arrogance has become divorced from the 'unenlightened' masses, the more difficulty it has had in coping with this task.

Under the conditions of globalization and technological revolution, capitalism acts increasingly as a destructive force, disrupting natural social bonds and relationships, including those that are essential for the stability of capitalism itself. The left, by contrast, is destined to become an integrating social force, counterposing to the logic of fragmentation its own logic of col-lectivism and solidarity. In relation to the technological achievements at the end of the century, the left has to throw down a new challenge to the capitalist structures within which technology is developing.

The left is afraid to speak of redistribution, when redistribution is becoming a question of life and death for society. Everything has to be redistributed from the top down – technology, resources, money, knowledge. At a certain stage, the thrust of development must no longer be 'onward and upward', but once again 'outward and in depth'. Now, however, everything at the 'uninteresting' middle levels is grinding to a standstill. So long as there is no growth at these levels, nothing moves downward. Nor can the education system cope. It remains oriented toward providing the quantity and quality of workers required now, and is thus constantly falling behind, since tomorrow more and better workers will be required. If these workers are to be provided, then not only will more students be needed, but also more teachers, and at the same time a more effective school system, along with more theatres and libraries, a more favourable environment for reproducing the labour power of intellectuals, and correspondingly, quite different values in society, different ideological demands, and so forth. In the 1960s and 1970s education was regarded as a value in itself. This was the result both of the overall advance of socialist values in the world, and of the struggle between the two systems. Education was developing not because firms needed qualified specialists (on the contrary, there was a surplus of them), but because millions of working-class families considered it important as a matter of principle to raise the social status of their children through education. As a political factor, education had considerably more importance than the economy. But it was precisely this democratic breakthrough in the West that created the conditions for the computer revolution, provided it with the necessary personnel, and gave rise to its key ideas. Paradoxically, from the moment when the computer became a factor in the global victory of capitalism in the Cold War, the social base of the technological revolution also began narrowing dramatically. This base was never particularly broad in the countries of the 'periphery', but now it is shrinking rapidly in the countries of the 'centre' as well. The importing from Russia of scientists and engineers is not just a modern-day form of the 'imperialist plunder' about which so much has already been said and written, but is also a sign of the acute internal problems which capitalist society is encountering in the most developed countries.

The loud noises which liberal leaders in the West, from British Prime Minister Tony Blair to American President Bill Clinton, are now uttering about the need for 'education and still more education' represent either pious hopes or outright demagogy. The priorities of education and those of the market are incompatible. Investing in education requires a massive redistribution of wealth, at the expense of the profits of the computer firms and even at the expense of investments in new technologies.

A renewal of the left depends on the readiness of leftists to challenge the prevailing norms and principles. These principles appear unshakeable precisely because no one has the resolve to dispute them. The logic of capitalism seems 'natural' because no one calls it into question. For all the monstrous problems and contradictions of the Soviet Union, so long as it existed there was empirical proof that another social logic was possible besides that of capitalism. In effect, the collapse of the Soviet system made the left forget everything it had known until then. Everything now has to be learnt over again, and there is little time available.

The movement has to be refounded and rebuilt so as to unite working people on the various technological 'floors' in the countries of the centre and the periphery. By encouraging social fragmentation, capital strengthens its hold over people, but at the same time it destroys the bases for the existence of society – of any society, including that of capitalism. The left has to recognize its responsibility as a force calling not only for a more just distribution of wealth and a more democratic state, but also for the preservation of society, of civilization as such.

The crisis of capitalism is becoming more and more acute. The information networks are increasingly overloaded with meaningless pseudo-information. Financial flows are in chaotic disorder. The players on the stock market are themselves increasingly confused, and now have only a poor understanding of the ever more complex rules of the game. The virtual economy is smothering the 'real sector', while finding at the same time that it cannot exist without it. The state is being called upon to take emergency measures in the fields of the economy and social welfare, at the same time as it is being stripped of its property, authority and sovereign rights. The people are being offered democracy on the condition that they renounce any real choice.

In such a situation, can the left really reconcile itself to the 'logic of the system'? If it can, then what is the point in the left existing at all?

Ultimately, all the problems have their roots in the historical limitations of capitalism. These problems will not be solved without a comprehensive transformation of society, in exactly the same way as the ills of the environment will not be cured no matter how many top-level meetings are held. In the nineteenth century people had faith in uninterrupted social progress. The shocks of the twentieth century have forced them to question this belief. But technical progress has gone ahead regardless, stopping neither for economic crises, nor wars, nor revolutions. The forces of production might collapse, but accumulated knowledge has made it possible to quickly restore what has been lost and to carry on. People have tried not to think about the fact that, in many ways, social progress has helped social and political contradictions to pile up.

This, however, has not always been the case. Human history knows of at least one period when accumulated technological knowledge has simply been lost, because the breakdown of society has made this knowledge meaningless. This is what happened when the Roman Empire collapsed. Five centuries were needed to make up the ground that had been lost.

The Roman state in its later years was an empire of arrogance. Even before this self-confidence was punished by the march of history, Christian preachers appeared in the markets and theatres, calling on people to change their ways and subdue their pride. In the end, of course, the destitute preachers became self-satisfied bishops, and pride triumphed yet again. But not for long; society had collapsed.

The left-wing politicians of the neo-liberal epoch are like those bishops of the late Roman Empire. They owe their success to their earlier radical preaching, but they themselves no longer believe in it. They lack the resolve either to act in line with their historical values, or to openly renounce them. But millions of people who encounter the vices of the system on a day-to-day basis are becoming more and more aggressively inclined. They are no longer prepared to restrain themselves. They need an alternative. They are ready to fight and win.

There is very little to admire in the really existing left. However, there are also reasons for hope. Even in the parties that went far to the right there is a growing leftist opposition. The leaderships are inevitably exposed to mounting pressure from the masses. And that creates a real political space for those who work for the radicalization of the left. Some of these oppositions will fail to achieve anything: some of them may be more successful. Many of the so-called 'socialist' parties are lost for socialism, but not all of them. Often the forces that challenge social democracy from the left are themselves gradually becoming social-democratized, but this is not always irreversible.

The left is entering on a period of historic re-foundation. Our success now depends on our ability to act according to our principles and reject the temptations of the system. Capitalism is stronger today than the left. This is no news for anyone. But history is full of examples when the weak defeated the strong. There were failures and errors and there will be even more failures and errors in the future. Nobody is perfect, especially in politics. But radicalization of the movement itself generates a momentum that pushes us towards the new frontiers. The time comes when intellectual and political courage is crucial. We must not be afraid of moving forward.

We on the left have been suffering defeats for so long, that we have got into the habit of it. We need to be broken of our bad habits.

It is time to sound the trumpets, and to go on the attack.

1

Does Trade Unionism Have a Future?

The 1980s were a difficult period for trade unions. Even in countries where workers' organizations had traditionally played a decisive role in political and social life, the labour movement suffered one setback after another. The lengthy strike by British coal miners in 1984 and 1985 ended in defeat. In Italy the trade unions were unable to defend the '*scala mobile*' – automatic indexation of wages that had been regarded as their most important gain of the 1970s. The alliance between the three main Italian trade union federations fell apart. In most other European countries, including those of Scandinavia, the influence of the trade unions was severely undermined. More and more often, the trade unions themselves figured in popular consciousness not as the embodiment of the might of organized labour, but as ineffectual, conservative, bureaucratized and in some cases corrupt formations.

By the mid-1990s there had been no substantial improvement.

The Crisis of Unionism

Defeats and retreats of labour in the 1980s and 1990s obliged sociologists, at first liberal ones but then leftists as well, to speak of a crisis of the world trade union movement or of a 'crisis of syndicalism'. Liberal ideologues set out to show that trade unions had outlived their time, along with old industrial technologies and economic relationships. There was simply no place for them in a world of global competition and free entrepreneurship. The leftists did not agree with this assessment, but could not deny that the trade unions had suffered an obvious decline.

The first symptom of this decline was a fall in the number of trade union members. In the United States union members accounted for 35.5 per cent of the workforce in 1945, but by 1994 this figure was only 15.5 per cent. Particularly alarming was the fact that as the union leaders themselves admitted, the unions were 'failing to implant themselves to a significant degree in the growing high-technology sectors'.[1] In France by the mid-1990s the proportion of workers organized in trade unions had fallen to less than 10 per cent. Even in Germany, where the trade union movement avoided serious setbacks during the 1980s, membership declined by more than a million people after the unification of the country. Significantly, this process was apparent not only in the former East Germany, where it might readily have been explained by the transformation of social relationships and by the collapse of the system of obligatory membership. Trade union membership also declined in the western provinces. In the view of union officials, the reason was 'a rapid rise in unemployment and a weakening of the attachment felt by individuals for large organizations – a process which sociologists term "individualization"'.[2] American union officials also complained that their organizations had become 'irrelevant to the overwhelming majority of unorganized workers in our country'.[3]

In reality, the causes of the crisis lie considerably deeper.

At an international conference held in Stockholm in June 1995, and aimed at helping to develop new trade union structures, it was noted that analogous processes were taking place in most developed countries. In the West, the 1980s and 1990s have been above all a time of enormous technological change. Computerization and robotization have brought a dramatic reduction of employment in many fields. At the same time, many trades have become devalued. Paradoxically, it is by no means always the case that the computerization of production imposes increased demands on the worker. On the contrary, the appearance of more modern equipment may mean that the level of qualifications required of workers may even fall. This means not only increased unemployment, but also a reduction in workers' self-esteem, and an increase in their dependence on employers. Employers themselves have less need of particular workers, who can very easily be replaced.

Common wisdom presents unions as an obstacle to technological change. That is not exactly so. Many scholars insist on the effectiveness of workers' input and unions participation in the successful introduction of technological innovation, while limiting job losses. Studies show that, 'there is not necessarily a conflict between upgrading the technological basis of the firm and keeping most of the workers, generally retraining them'. Further, 'firms with high levels of protection were also those with the highest change in innovation'.[4]

If this is so, the question is: why was innovation so often accompanied by job losses and union busting? The answer to this question is simple, though not very popular among the scholars. Although new technologies are not necessarily in conflict with job protection and unionization they provide capital with new effective options in the class struggle against organized labour. In that sense, and only in that sense, technological change really meant a historic defeat of the unions, at least in their current form.

Trade unions have always thought of themselves above all as organizations of the industrial working class. While the number of industrial workers in Western countries is shrinking, an increase is occurring in the number of people employed the area of services (often poorly paid and cruelly exploited). Employment is also increasing in the financial sector, and in the systems of management and marketing. Finally, more and more people are accepting part-time employment, working at home or performing work simultaneously for several employers. All these categories of workers have their particular interests and problems, but the traditional forms of trade union organization, oriented toward large-scale industry, do not suit them.

Trade unions are faced with such problems even in countries where the industrial working class is continuing to grow. In a survey of the trade union movement, the *Korea Times* notes that on the whole the growth of the economy should stimulate the labour movement. 'However', the newspaper remarks:

> diminishing [numbers of] blue-collar workers in dwindling manufacturing sectors and increasing number of temporary, part-time or dispatched [migrant] workers brought about a decline in the number of union members. This resulted in the shrinking of the unionization rate to 15.6 per cent in 1994 from 19.5 per cent in 1990 and 21 per cent in 1980.[5]

Overall, developments in South Korea have favoured the trade unions. Declining employment in some sectors has been accompanied by growth in others, while the country's economic success has ensured a strong position for the labour movement. The democratization of South Korean society has seen not only a broadening of trade union rights since 1987, but also a pronounced growth of wages. The latter have risen considerably faster than the increase in labour productivity. South Korea has entered the category of advanced industrial countries, and has come to share the problems typical of such states. The cost of labour power has become much higher than in less developed countries, even though, in technological terms, the local monopolies remain dependent on the West. Real estate prices have risen dramatically, credit has become excessively expensive and economic growth rates have started to slip. As in other advanced countries, South Korea's rulers have put their faith in globalization, and have begun trying to solve their problems by cutting wages and restricting trade union rights.

The trade union movements of Third World countries have also entered into crisis. In the mid-1990s the Filipino workers' leader Filemon Lagman was speaking of the inability of the trade unions to adapt effectively to the processes of globalization and economic development. 'Even the progressive wing of the workers' movement failed to upgrade the backwardness of trade unionism in this country.' According to Lagman, the Filipino trade union movement lacks a 'motive force', while locally based actions cannot make up for the lack of a strategy.[6]

A third factor in the crisis has been the decline of the 'welfare state'. During periods when ensuring the social welfare of citizens was considered a key task of the state both in the West and in the East, and governments and social systems vied to see who could provide greater benefits to the population, trade unions were perceived as vital national institutions, indispensable partners of the authorities and of the ruling class. With the beginning of the era of neo-liberalism and with the victory of the West in the Cold War, this situation has finally vanished into the past. The social revenge of the bourgeoisie has made dismantling the system of social welfare one of the authorities' main concerns. In this situation, trade unions are being transformed from partners of the state into 'obstacles to the implementation of reforms', or even into enemies.

The New Zealand researchers Raymond Harbridge and Anthony Honeybone note that changes in the policies of the state have themselves been a cause of the decline of trade unions.

All the causes of decline mentioned in the international literature. . . are evident in New Zealand, but they are not to be compared with the decisive role played by the state. Beginning in 1988, changes have occurred in the structure of the labour market, but the consequences of this have not been particularly significant. Public opinion and the values of society have indeed become more individualistic, but there are no signs of a growth in anti-trade union sentiment. In our view, the organizational strategy of the trade unions has been weak because it has been rooted in a particular system. The majority of New Zealand trade unions have still to work out a strategy for organization and growth that corresponds to the new conditions.[7]

The membership and influence of the trade unions have fallen with particular rapidity in the private sector. This, just as much as the traditional socialist ideology, has driven the trade unions to resist privatization. But in most cases such struggles have ended in defeat, weakening the movement still further.

The ideological crisis of the left has been another factor weakening the trade unions. Although it was only the communists who suffered defeat in the years from 1989 to 1991, while the social democrats and radicals were able to speak of their theoretical vindication, the collapse of communism in practice struck a mighty blow against all types of left ideology and all forms of the workers' movement, including trade unions. If support for the free market represents 'the only true ideology', then all forms of workers' organization are doomed, since trade unions and similar bodies limit free competition on the labour market. If individual workers are convinced that market competition provides them with the maximum chances of betterment, they will not only be uninterested in taking out union membership, but will also regard trade unions as their enemies.

The globalization of the economy is creating new problems and weakening the traditional links between workers and their representatives. 'The transferring of trade union action into the new European space, and then into the world space, means that it loses a good deal of its strength along the way', writes the French trade unionist Hubert Bouchet.

The globalization of enterprises has distanced the representatives of wage workers from the centres of decision-making, to the point where the latter have become almost 'virtual'. It is now increasingly rare for trade unionists to come face to face with a real director. The person negotiating on behalf of the employers, even if present on the local scene, is most often the representative of a geographically inaccessible power. In this way the vicious game of competition, conducted blindly by an 'invisible hand' that has gone crazy, extends its rule.[8]

The Post-Soviet Trade Unions

The trade unions in Eastern Europe and the former USSR are also experiencing enormous difficulties. Here technological innovation is not in any sense to blame for the crisis of industry, for the dramatic falls in production or for growing unemployment. New technologies are being introduced, but not on anything like the scale seen in the West. The social crisis has been provoked by the breaking of links within the productive process, by the shrinking of the market for local producers, and by the plunder of state property. Together with political and legal instability, these factors have brought about a paralysis of investment.

Trade unions are unable to adapt to the new political system and the new situation. They lack experience of defending hired workers in the conditions of the market. Nor are they able to make use of the market experience of the West, due to a lack of genuine market relations. To paraphrase Lenin, the labour movement in these countries suffers both from capitalism and from its inadequate development.

Moreover, in most of the countries of the former Soviet bloc a fierce rivalry is occurring between the 'old' organizations and 'alternative' trade unions which arose on the wave of the democratic movement of the 1980s.

It is significant, however, that despite all these problems a high level of trade union membership has survived among the workers in most of these countries. Even in Lithuania, Estonia, Hungary, the Czech Republic and Poland, where trade union membership declined more rapidly in 1989 and 1990 than the regional average, a larger percentage of the workforce remained unionized than in Britain or Germany, not to mention France or Spain.[9]

Against expectations, the traditional trade unions in the countries of Eastern Europe have weathered the crisis much better than the 'alternative' ones. This has been obvious not only in Russia or Hungary, where the 'alternative' trade unions have never been a mass force throughout the country as a whole (particular sectors of the economy may be an exception here). In Poland and Bulgaria, where powerful 'alternative' union federations arose and played important roles in the democratization of society, the situation has been analogous. As Czech experts note in a report on the trade unions of the region, 'the leaders of the old trade unions consider themselves to be in the centre of political life, while the leaders of Solidarnosc feel themselves to have been cast onto its periphery'.[10]

However, the struggle between old and new trade unions in most countries is receding gradually into the past. Especially at the local level, joint union actions are becoming more and more commonplace. There is an increasing understanding that, in trying to weaken one another, the trade unions are merely strengthening the hands of the state and of the employers. No less important is the gradually spreading understanding that in the new conditions both old and new trade unions are in need of reforms. It is quite clear that the trade union movement, like society in general in these countries, has not yet taken on its stable, definitive forms. The future holds not only fierce struggles between various forces, but also important structural changes.

Old unions remained corporatist and bureaucratized organizations, often with corrupt leadership. Feeling weak they preferred to put forward modest demands. 'We are not talking here about the welfare state, but about a minimum social justice', declared the leadership of the National Trade Union Alliance (OPZZ) in Poland, 'about exerting some restraint on the excessive enrichment of the few at the expense of the majority.'[11] New unions lack tradition or have the 'wrong' one. They remain anti-communist and spontaneous, unable to develop long-term strategies. Some of them moved from ultra-liberal to far left positions, as happened with the Independent Union of Miners, the strongest 'new' union in Russia. But, even turning to the left, they do not have either a new concept of class struggle or a clear vision of their own role in it.

At the same time, most observers agree that the trade unions in Eastern Europe are surviving, and in some cases even making up lost ground. 'Unfortunately, the sparseness of information on the goals and problems of the trade unions has meant that only a few political and economic leaders appreciate the depth and scope of this movement', note the authors of the report cited earlier.

> Despite the decline in popularity of the trade unions, resulting either from the beginning of the reforms or from the economic decline, the workers' movement in the countries of Eastern Europe is beginning to acquire an increasingly distinct shape, which will correspond to the needs of the coming century.[12]

Although in post-communist Eastern Europe the unions in general failed to do their job, some very important labour struggles did take place. Spontaneous protest of the Russian miners during the 'summer of discontent' in 1998 posed a serious threat to the Yeltsin regime and forced it to correct its social policies. In Romania a year later the miners' march to the capital really rocked the country. The scale of police repression that followed showed how frightened the rulers of the country were. Thousands of workers were beaten by the police and hundreds were arrested. Miners' leader Miron Cozma was sentenced to 18 years in prison for organizing mass protests which were characterized by the authorities as 'similar to an act of terrorism'.[13]

South Korean Activism

A still more striking contrast with the West is evident when we examine the processes occurring in the countries of the Third World and 'new industrial states'. While trade union membership in the West has been shrinking, unions in the non-Western world have been growing. In South Korea, despite all the problems confronting the labour movement, total union membership in 1990 stood at 1,886,000, or more than a quarter of the total number of hired workers. Under the relatively harsh political regime, the central organs of the trade unions were dependent on the government. This obliged them to be extremely moderate in their demands. But the workplace organizations were gradually radicalizing.

Democratization, which began in the late 1980s, created new possibilities for building the trade unions. During the 1970s and the first half of the 1980s, the level of strike activity in the country was extremely low. But in the second half of the 1980s the situation changed dramatically.

The *Korea Times* notes a sharp increase in the number of labour conflicts during the years from 1990 to 1997, at the same time as the number of trade unions ceased to grow. This relatively favourable situation for the labour movement resulted from the fact that the rapidly developing economy experienced constant shortages of skilled labour power. The trade unions, under the control of the authorities, could not take advantage of these opportunities. The number of 'wildcat' strikes grew dramatically, and the labour movement became politicized. In Korea as in other countries undergoing accelerated industrialization during the 1970s and 1980s, the development of trade unions was linked closely to the process of democratization. As the *Korea Times* notes, the beginning of the transition to democracy in 1987 'was a turning point in Korea industrial relations'.[14] Despite obvious efforts by the establishment to 'tame' the labour movement and turn it into an instrument of corporate rule, the radicalization of the workers went ahead ineluctably as economic growth slowed. The experience of collective action that had been accumulated during the struggle for democratization drove workers to put forward new demands, and ultimately created the preconditions for the emergence of independent political organizations. The increase in strike activity was accompanied by the massive growth of the new Korean Council of Labour Unions (*Minju Nochong*), whose rise was closely linked to the movement for democratic rights. Sociologists studying the labour movement in present-day South Korea note that the prevailing tendency is toward the growth of trade union membership and the democratization of the unions themselves; these are turning into more radical and independent organizations.[15]

The ruling groups in South Korea promised to meet the demands of the workers and to review the legislation restricting the right to strike and to organize trade unions. The unions in turn were urged by the Korean establishment to 'discard the principle of confrontation and struggle', and to 'develop a formula based on participation and cooperation'. The conservative official Federation of Korean Trade Unions (*Minchu Nochong*) and the left-wing Korean Council of Labour Unions, it was argued, needed to be merged into one.[16]

In fact, nothing has worked out as the authorities promised. In December 1996 the government forced through parliament a law on labour relations that restricted workers' rights. Hundreds of thousands of workers then downed tools in response to a call from the still 'illegal' Korean Council of Labour Unions. In January they were joined by the official Federation of Korean Trade Unions. Neither acts of repression against workers' leaders, nor threats of court prosecutions and lockouts were able to halt the strike. The protests continued for twenty days, reaching their peak on 15 January. Among the strikers were car workers, shipbuilders, manufacturing workers, hospital staff, television workers, public servants, bus and taxi drivers, and bank employees. 'New' and 'traditional' layers of the workforce, industrial and service workers were drawn equally into struggle, since their common interests were affected. President Kim Young-Sam was eventually forced to make concessions, sending the law back to parliament for 'reworking' and revoking the order for the arrest of trade union leaders.

The Asian crisis of 1997–98 not only put strong pressures on the workers but provoked new confrontations between militant unions and the elites accepting neo-liberal remedies for this crisis. Korean mainstream economists agree that neo-liberal restructuring will force 'painful sacrifices on workers – hardships in the form of protracted recession, massive unemployment, the lowering of real wages and living standards, aggravation of work conditions, and a weakening of labor power'. What worries the economists most, however, is the fact that these policies 'may cause social unrest, with the possibility that the hoped for reforms may experience a setback'.[17] Facing increasing pressure from the entrepreneurs, South Korean unionists understood the necessity of a political response. Right after the successful strike a discussion started in the labour movement about the need for a party, and already by 1997–99 some steps had been made in this direction.

As the Paris newspaper *Le Monde Diplomatique* observed:

These workers who had been held up to European wage-earners as models of flexibility and docility (characteristics that were more the result of militarized socio-economic relations than of a concern for competitiveness) suddenly appeared in the vanguard of the revolt against ultraliberal globalization.[18]

And David McNally in *Monthly Review* was even more resolute. While in the West labour unions are in decline, in the New Industrial Countries they are on the rise. 'But it's not just numbers that matter here. The working class throughout East Asia has also developed forms of militancy and self-organization that often put western labor movements to shame.'[19]

African Militancy

The history of trade unions in South Africa also illustrates the links between globalization, the struggle for democracy and the new wave of the labour movement in the countries of the capitalist periphery during the 1980s. In 1985 the majority of organizations of black workers combined to form the Congress of South African Trade Unions (COSATU). At the time of its formation, COSATU consisted of 34 affiliated unions with a total of 462,000 members. Over the next ten years COSATU's membership tripled, reaching 1,260,000.[20] Between 1979 and 1993 the total number of trade union members in South Africa increased from 701,758 to 2,470,481 people. In 1979 only 15.3 per cent of the people employed in industry were organized in trade unions; by 1993 this figure had reached 57.98 per cent. The growth of the trade unions significantly outstripped the increase in the workforce. In 1994 the number of trade union members in the country fell slightly, reflecting a general decline in the number of people employed in industry.[21]

As the researcher and ideologue of the South African trade union movement Karl von Holdt has observed, COSATU was faced with two simultaneous tasks. On the one hand, the trade unions became a powerful element in the struggle for democracy. They not only contributed to the democratization of society, but also undermined the apartheid regime at the enterprise level. On the other hand, the organizations making up COSATU, like trade unions throughout the world, set out to win collective agreements that secured wage increases and favourable working conditions. The main achievement of the trade unions, however, was that they allowed workers to feel their strength and to defend their dignity. Mass workers' actions led to 'uncontrollability and insubordination in the workplaces – and not only there – thus showing the rulers of South Africa that maintaining the apartheid system any longer was impossible'.[22] These actions were aimed to a significant degree at achieving the political and moral self-affirmation of the workers; often, they even conflicted with the immediate tasks of trade unions that were engaged in negotiating collective agreements. In some cases the spontaneous resistance by workers to the prevailing order acquired such scope that as von Holdt recognized, 'the trade union organization itself became ungovernable'.[23]

Within the trade union movement, fierce arguments flared between 'populists' who saw the main task of COSATU as lying in its pursuit of the general democratic struggle, and 'workerists' who insisted that the trade unions had first and foremost to carry out their immediate function: struggling for the interests of workers on the job, while at the same time developing socialist perspectives. Researchers have noted a striking similarity between this discussion and the debates which raged within the Russian labour movement in the early years of the century and in the Polish Solidarity trade union in 1980 and 1981.[24]

In the new South Africa the COSATU trade unions are having to define their role afresh. They are turning into an extremely important national institution, playing a huge role in the implementation of the Reconstruction and Development Programme. Mechanisms of social partnership are taking the place of confrontation, and the trade unions are participating in the adoption of decisions together with the government and the management of large state and private companies. Large numbers of trade union activists have filled out the state structures. About 60 prominent trade union leaders have become members of parliament. Trade union functionaries have made the shift to government organizations and company management structures in such numbers that the workers' organizations are unable to find adequate replacements for them. There is even talk of a 'massive brain drain' and of a 'cadre crisis' in COSATU.[25]

The problems which the trade unions face in present-day South Africa are the fruit largely of the labour movement's successes. This, of course, does not mean that 'final' victory has been achieved, or that the 'era of struggle' has been replaced by an epoch of 'constructive collaboration' with a renewed elite. On the contrary, the main contradictions giving birth to conflicts in society remain unresolved. The policies of the 'progressive' government, that was established with the direct support of the trade unions and the left, have by no means been oriented toward defending the interests of workers. The authorities have sought to win the trust of the monopolies and to join in the process of globalization, sacrificing the interests of their own social base. The labour movement has had no choice but to resist. Researchers note that the level of strike activity in the country did not fall after the democratic elections of 1994. 'In practice, workers are demanding that the changes occurring in the political sphere should be extended to the workplace.'[26] The trade unions are thus faced with continuing an active struggle, while at the same time making use of the new opportunities for collaboration with the authorities.

A strengthening of the social role of the trade unions is not only to be seen in the Republic of South Africa. Similar processes can be observed in other African countries. Researchers note that during the 1980s and 1990s trade unions have become an important democratizing factor in Zambia and Ghana. The official trade union federations have not only won significant autonomy from the authorities, but, to a significant degree, have also influenced the general process of change, 'altering the relationship of forces to the advantage of civil society'.[27] In Swaziland in 1994 mass strikes made it possible to speak of a turning point in the history of the country's labour movement. As researchers have recognized, a national strike in support of 27 demands advanced by the Federation of Trade Unions of Swaziland dramatically altered the situation in the country, 'giving the workers confidence in resisting the authorities and the entrepreneurs'. Significantly, the demands of the unions included not only the legalization of strikes and amendments to labour legislation, but also repealing the ban on the activity of political parties, as well as freedom of association, of unions and of the press.[28]

It is important to note that most trade union federations in Africa are encountering problems analogous to those in Eastern Europe. Privatization is going ahead, while a centralized economy and a one-party system are being replaced by an orientation to a free market along lines recommended by the International Monetary Fund. However, this is not leading to a fall in trade union membership. In Zimbabwe trade unions organized massive protests against neo-liberal policies.[29] The Organization of Workers of Mozambique (OTM) also strengthened itself through struggles. With the government moving to the right, 'workers are joining trade unions in order to organize themselves and defend their rights and socio-professional interests'.[30]

Third World Workers Form Fighting Unions

An impressive growth in the size, radicalism and combativeness of the trade union movement has also occurred in Brazil. In 1983 radical labour leaders established a new trade union federation, the Central Union of Workers (CUT). Later, more moderate union leaders united in the General Confederation of Workers, taking as their model the American AFL-CIO.[31] By the end of the 1980s the CUT, together with the Workers' Party which is closely associated with it, had become the largest social force in the country.

In the mid-1990s analogous processes began occurring in Indonesia. The industrial workforce in Indonesia is growing rapidly, and the formation of a modern working class is being accompanied, despite repression, by the appearance of increasingly influential mass trade union organizations putting forward radical demands. During 1997 mass demonstrations against the Suharto dictatorship were led by the Indonesian Centre for Workers' Struggle (PPBI), which is affiliated to the People's Democratic Party (PRD). The latter is accused by the authorities of being 'a reincarnation of the Indonesian Communist Party'.[32]

The unity between workers and students in Indonesia of the 1990s shows an impressive resemblance to the alliance between the revolutionary intelligentsia and industrial proletariat in 1905 Russian Revolution. After the fall of Suharto the struggle continued – this time against the IMF-sponsored austerity policies. The labour movement in Indonesia is much weaker than in some neighbouring countries, writes American scholar David McNally. 'But in the context of police and military repression, the militant determination of Indonesian workers is nothing short of inspiring. And in the aftermath of the popular movement that toppled Suharto, workers' organizations are becoming more confident and self-assertive.'[33]

In the Philippines in 1996 a massive 'tax revolt' broke out, with trade union activists playing the decisive role. The new rise in the labour movement was linked with the political radicalization of the trade unions and a growing trend towards unification. The radical National Confederation of Labor (NCL) was set up, and workers' leaders at the local level established the Fraternity of Union Presidents of the Philippines (KPUP). The growth in activity by the trade union movement took place against the background of important changes among Filipino leftists. Throughout the 1980s the main anti-capitalist forces in the country remained the Stalinist-Maoist Communist Party and the New People's Army, which were conducting armed struggle against the government. In 1993 the overwhelming majority of communists who were active in large cities, and about half the members of the party overall, announced a break with the party's earlier policies. From then on the main task became establishing a mass legal movement, which would not only take part in the struggle for power, but also participate in the day-to-day defence of workers' interests. The result of this process was the rise of the movement Solidarity of the Filipino Workers (BMP).

Far Eastern Economic Review observed that this 'could lead to the rebirth of a militant trade union movement in the country or even a leftist party that could openly contest elections'.[34] The links between the BMP and the trade unions allowed left activists to employ a variety of methods simultaneously. BMP leader Filemon 'Popoy' Lagman notes:

> The emergence of the KPUP, NCL and BMP signals the all-out effort of a new breed of labor leaders and organizations whose aim is to reinvent the labor movement in the Philippines and radically change the structures and complexion of trade unionism in this era of imperialist neoliberal globalization. The NCL and the KPUP are basically trade union organizations with parallel aims of advancing the unification of the labor movement. The NCL does its efforts from 'above', advancing the unification movement by transforming itself into a 'confederation' and advocating the unification of the major labor blocs into one trade union centre. The KPUP, on its part, is a grass-roots movement of local unions pushing for trade union unity from 'below', developing itself into a working class brotherhood of local union presidents cutting across organizational and political affiliations.

> The BMP, on the other hand, 'is a revolutionary socialist organization of the working class, aspiring to develop itself as a motive force within the trade union movement'.[35]

The examples listed clearly have a great deal in common. Trade unions are growing and radicalizing in states where a rapid development of traditional industry is under way, and where at the same time a mass struggle for political democracy is unfolding. It is clear that the trade union movement in these countries has been spawned by the democratic needs of the population no less than by the growth of industry and of the 'classical' working class.

New Social Unionism in Europe

It would be a mistake to suppose that trade unions are maintaining or strengthening their positions only in countries on the periphery of present-day world capitalism. It is significant that, despite abrupt technological changes, trade union membership has fallen scarcely at all in Canada and several other Western countries. While membership has declined sharply in Britain and France, trade union organizations have maintained a stable membership base in Germany, and in the Scandinavian countries there has even been growth. Between 1970 and 1990 the proportion of unionized workers in Norway increased from 51.4 to 56 per cent, in Sweden from 67.7 to 82.5 per cent, in Denmark from 60 to 71.4 per cent, and in Finland from 51.4 to 72.2 per cent.[36] It is noteworthy that the countries concerned are among the most developed in Europe, and that, throughout the years in question, intensive technological modernization was taking place. The decline in the industrial workforce in the Scandinavian countries was just as abrupt as in France or Britain. But not only was a collapse of the trade unions avoided, but the shift of workers out of industry was accompanied by a strengthening of the trade unions in the service sector. The dramatic difference between the situations in Canada and the US also shows that the fate of the trade unions depends not only on the prevailing economic trends, which are quite similar in both countries, but also on the political situation and on the strategies that hold sway within the labour movement itself.

The crisis of the trade unions in Britain began long before the widespread introduction of new technology in the mid-1980s, and to a great degree was predetermined by the unions' own organizational and cultural problems. The advent of new technologies simply made these problems more obvious and painful.

The defeat suffered by the trade unions in their struggle against the Conservative government of Margaret Thatcher, Will Hutton considers, was predetermined by the fact that finding themselves in bitter confrontation with the authorities, the unions 'were more like professional associations and the old guilds than the shock troops of the working class'.[37] Hutton concludes that what was needed was a more responsible trade unionism, but the directly opposite conclusion can also be drawn: that a more radical, class-based approach was indispensable. The positions of the British trade unions were undermined by the policies of the Thatcher government, policies which were openly directed against the labour movement. Not only 'objective processes', but also pressures from the ruling class were behind the crisis.

As Anna Pollert writes in *Socialist Register*:

> Looking across the spectrum from those industries actually privatized, to services still in state hands but increasingly operating under competitive imperatives, there is evidence that growing exposure to 'market discipline' is strengthening managerial prerogatives and undermining a former consensus-forming pattern of public sector industrial relations.[38]

In the course of the 1990s employers and the authorities have unleashed offensives against the trade unions in practically all European countries. But their successes have by no means been universal. The decline of the French trade unions did not prevent them from scoring a decisive victory over the government in December 1995. This strike not only gave the labour movement back the self-confidence it had lost, but also proved that the 'objectively essential' and seemingly irresistible wave of neo-liberal restructuring could in fact be stopped. The attempt by the Juppe government to review the historically established status of public sector workers aroused massive resistance, not only among the workers directly affected. Society realized that the 'Juppe plan' was not just another bureaucratic measure, but involved 'historic changes to the relations between hired workers, the state and employers'.[39] Former left-wing intellectuals who had tried to prove that resistance was useless under the conditions of glob-alization were left with egg on their faces. The few radicals who had held fast to their positions were exultant. 'One has the impression that behind the problems with social welfare, pensions and education there stands a new historic choice for society. In one way or another, society is changing.'[40] The newspaper *Le Monde* described the December 1995 strike as 'the first revolt against globalization'.[41] In reality, the revolt was far from being the first. Much more important was the fact that it was successful.

The change was more psychological and ideological than political. 'Indeed, future historians may treat it as an ideological turning point', writes Daniel Singer in his book *Whose Millennium*?

> What momentarily caused panic within the establishment was that its usual propaganda – you must accept the world as it is, with Maastricht, the, markets, the IMF and all – had no effect whatsoever on the mounting movement. The plain reply of the protesters was: if that is the future you offer us and our children, to hell with your future![42]

This time society intuitively understood the link between the survival of the public sector and the existence of social welfare and civil rights for all citizens. In the months from October to December the corporate movement that had existed earlier was transformed into a class movement. France not only gave the whole world another practical lesson in class struggle, but also showed how the content of class struggle was changing, how collective actions were giving birth to a new class consciousness.

The movement reached its height in December, when strikes and protest marches engulfed the whole country. The working class not only proved that it remained an important social and political force, but also that common demands could be formulated which united the traditional industrial workers with broad layers of workers in the 'post-industrial' sector. 'It became obvious that this working class is not solely made up of "middle aged, blue collar white men", as the stereotyped image of trade union membership would have one think.' The movement had a comprehensive character.

> At the marches, there was a visible spontaneous unity between unionized and non-unionized workers, between different trade unions, between workers from entirely different sectors of the economy. Also present were contingents from groups of the

unemployed and the homeless, as well as students and small groups of organized immigrant workers.[43]

Organized labour was again playing the key role in the movement, despite all the assertions that its time had passed. Moreover, a trend towards unity from below had appeared. Moderate leaders who had argued that resisting globalization was impossible discovered that their own base-level organizations were thinking and acting differently. December of 1995 prepared the ground for the electoral victory of the left in France two years later. For socialist leaders that victory came as a surprise. It is clear that something changed in the minds of the people. It became clear that the policies of globalization could be defeated.

A paradoxical but quite natural result of globalization has been the fact that struggles by workers in various parts of the world are more and more often taking place simultaneously, and are becoming more similar in many ways. The strikes in France and South Korea had different causes, but developed according to a single scenario. In both cases demands that originally were perceived as 'corporate' were later recognized by the bulk of the population as having a general democratic character. In this way, a new basis for solidarity arose. Unity was achieved not through moderation and compromise but, on the contrary, thanks to the fact that a tough position on the part of the strikers had won support in society. Despite the initially tough position of the authorities, the workers' determination to achieve their goals whatever the cost changed the situation. The more aggressively the authorities behaved, the greater public sympathy for the strikers became.

Changing the Concept of Unionism

The psychological significance of the events in France and South Korea was enormous. In 1998 Russian miners also showed their strength, blocking the roads in Siberia and forcing the government to pay wage arrears, though this time union leaders played little if any role in the struggles. Some of the strike leaders were soon elected as new union officials. A successful strike by United Parcel Service workers in America has shown that multinational corporations are not invincible.

After two decades of failures the organized labour movement showed that it could emerge victorious from a head-on clash with the authorities. The movement also proved that measures that were supposed to be 'objectively essential under conditions of globalization' could be unceremoniously reversed if the political will for this was present.

Analysing the events of the 1960s and 1970s, the historian Donald Sassoon posited the existence of a 'European-wide strike cycle'.[44] Sassoon was unable to suggest what might account for this cyclical motion, since the rises and declines in labour activism did not coincide either with the business cycle, or with the dynamic of inflation. In fact, the class struggle has its own dynamic, which depends on socio-economic processes, on the evolution of workers' organizations, and on the spontaneous development of workers' consciousness. During the second half of the 1990s a new generation, that has not experienced the shock of previous failures and is free from old ideological stereotypes, has entered the labour market. The workers have begun to overcome the demoralization and confusion brought by the changes of the 1980s. At the same time, inevitable leadership changes have begun within the trade union structures themselves. The crisis of the trade union movement in the developed capitalist countries, which reached its logical limit when the very existence of workers' organizations came under question, eventually acted as a powerful stimulus for renewal. Globalization impelled this process forward.

In 1995 the old leadership of the American AFL-CIO labour federation was forced to retire, and radical changes began even in this preserve of bureaucracy and conservatism. Important resources were devoted to organizing new groups of workers, and a generation of young radicals who had received the chance to prove their mettle entered the trade unions. In 1996, perhaps half a century later than might have been expected, a Labor Party was founded.

Not surprisingly, these developments provoked alarm in the big-business press and the corporate and political establishment.

As one of the reformers, Oil, Chemical and Atomic Workers' International Union President Robert E. Wages, wrote:

> The verdict is still out in many of the changes being made at the AFL-CIO. However the jury is unanimous in finding the

labor movement *guilty* of changing the perception that it had passed on to that great unorganized shop in the sky. Things have changed, and once again we find ourselves being attacked in ever increasing bitter diatribes. This all suggests that the labor movement is once again relevant.[45]

Comparing the experience of various countries also allows one to give a more definite answer to the question of the future prospects for trade unions. It is quite obvious that the theories pointing to the progressive demise of the trade union movement do not correspond to reality. But in order to play an appropriate role in a changing society, trade union organizations are going to have to change as well.

Solidarity acquires another meaning in the times of globalization when workers must be organized and struggles coordinated internationally. However, it is totally wrong to expect a new militant response to globalization to emerge at the international level without radical transformation and strengthening of the labour movement on the national level. 'Even national battles depend on the militancy gained in local conflicts', writes Daniel Singer. 'It is naive to assume that, say, German or French unions, passive and defensive on their own soil, will suddenly show a fighting spirit as soon as the confrontation is extended to the European Union.'[46]

Historically, trade unions have not only been a form of combination of industrial workers, but also the largest organizations of working people, representing their interests in the democratic system. As organs ensuring that workers take part in social, economic and political decision-making at the most diverse levels, trade unions today are not only necessary, but also irreplaceable. The growing complexity of society simply increases the need for them. Under present-day conditions, however, trade unions will be able to fulfil their role only if their own structures reflect the processes occurring in the world of labour. It is clear that the problems which the trade union movement confronts are not only external. Centralized, bureaucratized and in some cases completely undemocratic, the structures of the traditional trade unions are becoming an anachronism. If the trade unions are to become genuinely representative organs, they still need to pass through a difficult and perhaps lengthy process of self-reform.

The social base of the trade union organizations also needs to undergo changes. The question remains unresolved of whether the trade unions should include unemployed workers, pensioners and worker-owners. Some currents in Western Europe see this as the way to overcome the crisis. In particular, the Italian Union of Labour (UIL) sees itself not so much as a traditional 'workers' trade union' as a 'trade union of citizens'. Often the trade union leaders themselves, rejecting the traditional model of 'proletarian syndicalism', see their role as consisting not so much in organizing workers as in competently representing their interests. When such an approach is adopted, the role of trade union activism declines sharply, but the influence of the trade unions in society remains relatively great; this is confirmed by surveys of public opinion and by elections to enterprise councils.[47]

Broadening the social base of the trade unions makes sense if it is combined with a militant strategy aimed at defending important common interests. Even before the events of December 1995 the oldest French trade union federation, the General Confederation of Labour (CGT), had gradually begun to recover its position. In the late 1980s it had been under substantial pressure from the moderate Democratic French Confederation of Labour (CFDT) and from independent unions, but by the mid-1990s the situation had shifted in its favour. Leaders of the CGT spoke with pride of 'influence regained'.[48] The reason was precisely the 'conservatism' and 'traditionalism' of the CGT, which had held fast to class positions and actively resisted the 'indispensable reforms'. This did not by any means signify that the CGT unions had remained unchanged. On the contrary, the union leaders understood clearly that the world of labour had lost its former homogeneity, and that a new, more flexible type of organization was required. A greater degree of federalism and decentralization was essential. The unifying principle was no longer a single class culture and professional ethic, but 'inter-professional convergences'.[49] This policy yielded its fruits in 1995 and 1996.

The transformation of trade unions into specialized structures ensuring that the interests of labour are represented in the system of decision-making cannot in any way be considered an ideal prospect. The strength of 'classical trade unionism' consisted precisely in the fact that it combined the functions of representation and self-organization, while simultaneously playing an important political and cultural role in society.

A purely representative trade union will inevitably rest on a passively loyal membership, and is unlikely to succeed in becoming a force facilitating profound changes. It is precisely the representative tendency that is dominant today in the trade union movement of Eastern Europe and a significant part of the West. It would, however, be premature to state that this is where the future of the trade unions lies.

Another crucial problem for the trade unions is the need to overcome the divisions between 'white-collar' and 'blue-collar' workers. It is obvious that organizing the staff of decentralized research organizations, or office workers in the modern banking system, requires methods that are different from those needed to unite workers on a production line. But it is no less obvious that, as hired workers, specialists sitting in front of computers also have common interests and need to be organized.

The 1990s have become a time of gradual growth and strengthening of the trade union movement in the sectors of the economy based on new technologies. Here new forms of organization and activity have arisen. In the area of new technologies the struggle by workers for their rights can be successful only if it is combined with the defence of the interests and rights of users. Unlike the old service sector, where the interests of the consumer and of the worker were often in opposition to one another, in information systems the producers and users are closely linked to one another. 'Communication workers in particular are vital to communication activism, as they are in the center of the maelstrom', notes the American researcher Robert W. McChesney.

In Canada and parts of Europe the communication unions are the ones who are leading the fight against privatization and deregulation of telecommunications. These unions recognize that traditional campaigns to protect jobs and benefits in the short run may enjoy some success, but they do nothing to address the longterm trajectory of the industry, which is fiercely anti-labor. They are moving therefore toward a position of providing a broader vision of communication where the workers and not the investors are the representatives of the public interest. Communication unions are forming alliances with consumer and community groups to advocate a socially responsive vision of a non-market telecommunication system. This model of progressive social unionism may be worthy of emulation by all the labor movement, not just those unions connected to the communication industries.[50]

New technologies require new organizational forms. When transnational corporations use the mobility of capital as a weapon for lowering wages, it becomes essential to unite workers not on the basis of enterprises and workshops, but according to technological sectors or regions. Also essential are transnational labour unions. The first organizations of this kind already exist in North America and in the countries of the former Soviet Union, but they are often bureaucratized and corrupt.

The trade unions also need to reject the traditional counterposing of collective bargaining to individual contracts. In reality, neither of these excludes the other, since the general conditions fixed in each individual contract can and must be the object of collective bargaining. A great deal of work also lies ahead in the area of organizing and defending the interests of part-time workers.

The democratization of the trade unions is becoming an indispensable condition for their effective functioning. It is no longer possible to rely on the automatic loyalty of large numbers of people dispersed not only among various enterprises but also across different countries, and the proliferating bureaucracy is at risk of losing control over its own structures. Solidarity can only be guaranteed through intensive horizontal links and through common participation in decision-making.

The trade unions have to develop in a context in which the world of hired labour has become much less homogeneous than in the days of 'classical' unionism. We are not just concerned here with the growing diversity of technologies, qualifications and types of employment. The numbers of working women have grown rapidly, and immigrants have come to play an expanded role in the labour markets of developed countries. The working class of the late nineteenth century consisted primarily of white males engaged in physical labour. Modern-day workers may be Christians or Muslims, men or women, white or black; they may work with a computer or with a spade. Modern trade unions have to find what unites these people, have to become organs reconciling their interests. In the conditions of the late twentieth century the democratization of the trade unions has become impossible without their feminization, without changes to their culture, traditions and membership base.

The American Marxist scholar, Peter Meiksins, writes:

> Overcoming these kinds of divisions, forging harmonious relations among workers from different racial and ethnic backgrounds, overcoming differences of status within the waged labor force, and unifying workers with different occupational experiences requires a real 'class' project. . . . Such a project would mean mounting a real challenge to the hegemony of capitalism, to its claim to be able to organize production in a rational effective way.[51]

The working class of the past not only created trade unions as a form of organized self-defence, it also transformed and created itself through the union struggles. It was not only the class that formed the unions and parties but also parties which helped to form and shape the class. Modern working masses need unions not only to protect their interests but, even more, to establish themselves as a social force.

It is no accident that in Sweden, against a background of profound crisis in the labour movement, researchers note the success of the trade union of municipal workers. This union was one of the first to confront these problems and to make a serious effort to find solutions to them. New approaches have appeared in the decentralization of the union, and in changes to its political culture. The union has rejected collective membership in the Social Democratic Party, which union members no longer regard as 'automatically' expressing their interests.[52]

It is significant that the 'self-reform' that has begun in the trade union movements of Norway and Denmark is proceeding in the same direction. The traditional ties to social democracy are growing weaker. At the same time, the overwhelming majority of activists consider it essential to maintain the centralization of the leadership as a guarantee of effective national solidarity actions, while simultaneously expanding the opportunities open to trade union bodies at the local level.[53]

The weakening of ties to social democracy does not by any means signify that the trade unions are becoming depoliticized, or that they are shifting to liberal positions. On the contrary, it seems that we are witnessing the first steps toward a 'new political unionism'. The essence of this lies in the fact that the trade unions are ready to intervene actively in politics from radical positions, relying less and less on the mediating function of the traditional workers' parties. The trade union activists themselves are remaining members of the social democratic organizations, or are joining more radical left parties such as the Socialist People's Party of Denmark, the Left Party of Sweden, and the Socialist Left Party of Norway. As members of these parties, they use them to advance the ideas and demands of their trade unions.

The traditional ideology of the labour movement assumed that centralization and discipline made workers stronger in the face of the class enemy. The history of the twentieth century shows that centralized structures have been used precisely in order to bind workers to a bureaucratic compromise that is against their interests. The new radical trade unionism is invariably linked to the idea of decentralization and democratization. This can be seen in Europe, Asia and Latin America. 'I believe that we have fallen into verticalism, into an excessive respect for hierarchies and for organic structures', representatives of the left wing of the Uruguayan trade unions declare. Decentralized labour organizations will inevitably reflect the radicalization of the masses. They simply have no alternative.

> There is no longer any room for a trade unionism of class conciliation, of social pacts, because there is no longer any room for a capitalism with a human face, for a beneficial, 'statist' capitalism and so on. Today we are talking about unemployment, but if we take any other problem, for example, corruption, which is also a world-wide phenomenon, we see that it can only be combated or neutralized through measures such as the abolition of bank secrecy which would amount to a fundamental restriction of the powers of speculative finance capital. Hence it is impossible to conceive of an effective trade unionism which does not plan consciously and concretely to struggle for social transformation.[54]

In Europe the ideology of trade unions also changes. A French labour activist Christophe Auguiton notes that after December 1995 in the unions you can see 'the emergence of the new radicalism, a return of the leftism, but very different from those of the 70s'.[55]

Finally, the globalization of the economy is forcing the trade unions to concern themselves with new forms of international solidarity. The decisive role here will be played not by contacts between leaders in various forums, but by the development of direct 'horizontal' links between trade union organizations and activists within the framework of one corporation or sector. Modern technology makes this possible. Even today one can speak of the birth of a system of global trade union communications. To a significant degree this is happening spontaneously, regardless of decisions taken by trade union hierarchs. Sooner or later this development will make its effects felt throughout the whole area of trade union organizing, creating new democratic possibilities.[56]

All this necessitates changes in the forms and methods of trade union work. It may be that this is a task for a new generation of trade union activists and leaders, who will have to find answers to the challenges posed by new circumstances.

2

Beyond Identities

The market economy is supposed to satisfy the needs of humanity, offering the consumer a choice of everything for which there is a demand, just as newspapers promise to publish all the news fit to print. But in the marketplace, the customer ceased long ago to be the central figure. Consumers are now no more than a 'necessary evil' in a world of competition between brand names and image-makers.

The less active a citizen is, the more he or she is transformed into a consumer of politics. Participatory democracy is replaced by a 'freedom of choice' resembling the 'freedom' of a customer in a supermarket. 'In today's consumer cultures, where style prevails as a dominant form of currency, style presents people with many ways of seeing and comprehending society', notes the American scholar Stuart Ewen. 'The extensive choice and variety of images, which enshrine the goods we may purchase, is regularly equated with a choice and variety in ideas and perspectives that we may hold or give voice to.'[1] The modern market constantly demands the appearance of new goods whose advantage lies precisely in their novelty. The concept of 'novelty' becomes critical, supplanting the earlier notion of 'quality'. The symbolic significance of an object is at least as important as its 'use value'. In a certain sense the acquiring of a prestige symbol as one's property becomes in itself the goal of consumption – the self-affirmation of the 'market' man or woman.

Changing Fashions

'Redundant diversity' is becoming a characteristic feature of the capitalist market. To the choice between goods is added a choice between advertising symbols, behind which might be a quite ordinary or familiar product. 'Redundant diversity' does not broaden consumer choice but restricts it, since the consumer loses the chance to make a free, competent decision. More and more often consumers come to depend on specialized intermediaries for help in orienting themselves in the market, or else they become subject to manipulation by producers, sellers and advertising experts. What is purchased is no longer a good, but a trade mark, an image, a reputation.

Something similar is happening in politics. The simple old formulae of 'class struggle', 'social transformation', 'solidarity' and 'popular power' are becoming 'old-fashioned' not because they are remote from the needs of present-day humanity, but because they are forced onto a subordinate level by new ideas formulated so as to accord exactly with the principles of modern advertising. New goods have to keep appearing constantly on the market, not because consumers need them (the consumers do not even know about them yet), but because the whole system of commercial propaganda would otherwise lose its motive force.

The more the field of ideas becomes a sphere of commerce, and the more it is penetrated by the criteria and demands of the market, the more kaleidoscopic are the shifts of ideological fashion. The left radicalism of the 1960s was not a mere whim of spoiled intellectuals, but it was quickly taken over and exploited by the market together with Beatles songs and mini-skirts. Various ideas had aroused mass enthusiasm before; this is a normal phenomenon of social life. Through embracing the dominant ideas, a person can more easily make a career, winning a prominent place in the ruling circles or, on the other hand, in the opposition. But it is only since the 1960s that political ideas have been drawn directly into the sphere of the market. On the one hand the market is becoming more and more 'virtual', while on the other ideology is increasingly conjunctural, in the literal rather than the figurative sense of the word.

Whether we like it or not, the ideological revolution of the 1960s provided the starting-point for this process. The ideas of that time were quickly forgotten by many of their supporters. The radicalism of students in revolt was replaced by the pragmatism of young professionals, and the call for social revolution by policies of critical coexistence with the system. The degeneration of social democracy and the disappearance of the revolutionary left helped ensure the success of a respectable bourgeois radicalism, reflecting the needs and tastes of the educated middle class.

Unlike earlier ideological trends, the new ones were not just assimilated rapidly by the market, but were oriented to the market from the very beginning. At the same time, there was a direct continuity between the liberating wave of the 1960s and the commercial pragmatism of the subsequent decades. The age of youth revolt gave rise to models and approaches that could be developed and combined, and on the basis of which fashionable ideas could be formulated again and again, just as fashion designers could reshape the 'classical' mini-skirt to the point where it was unrecognizable.

From the mid-1980s, the ideological craze became postmodernism. From painting and architecture this term was quickly transferred to sociology and politics. Postmodernism provided leftists with the chance to free themselves from the need for a complex strategy, for an integrated worldview, and for definitive evaluations. The idea of systemic change was abandoned. 'We do not share . . . a view that there is this one thing called *capitalism*, to be replaced by a clearly conceived alternative, socialism.'[2] There is no system; there are only practices, and these of course are in constant flux.

In essence, postmodernist ideological concepts are nothing other than a projection onto social and political life of the market situation of redundant diversity. The world is a colourful mosaic, and within the framework of the postmodernist approach the content can change like the view within a kaleidoscope. The old-fashioned socialist movement was fated to give way to new social movements, to feminism, to movements of oppressed minorities, to the whole spectrum of diverse initiatives that have been given the name of 'identity politics'. The ideology of social revolution was put off until the future, while self-affirmation allowed people to live in the present.

This did not signify a rejection of left politics as such. Leftists were simply urged to give their doctrines a new content that would make left radicalism more saleable on the market of ideas. The strong side of the postmodernist critique of Marxism consists in the fact that it shifts to the forefront real problems which in the old socialist theory remained in the background, where indeed they were generally hidden. Racial, ethnic and religious oppression are quite real, and cannot simply be dismissed as 'side effects of capitalism', even if the exploitation of labour underlies all of them. The oppression of women is just as real and just as multi-faceted. Finally, the world of labour is becoming less and less homogeneous, and old concepts of the 'working class' have therefore to be re-examined.

Identity Politics

It is hard to exaggerate the intellectual shock which socialists suffered as a result of the postmodernist critique. The victors seized the field of battle almost without resistance. But after finishing on top in the struggle against left-wing traditionalism, postmodernist ideology ran up against its own internal contradictions.

Identity politics became possible thanks to the ideological decay of socialism, as a result of which the only real alternative to the dominant neo-liberalism appeared to be a sort of radical liberalism. This was the natural outcome of the evolution of the part of the Western left intelligentsia that took a critical attitude to capitalism, but which was either unwilling or unable to unite with the mass workers' movement. The intelligentsia itself was not always to blame for this. Since the 1950s, collaboration of this type has become more and more difficult to set in motion. The obstacles have included both persecution from the authorities, who have succeeded in isolating 'reds' from large sectors of society in the United States, and the anti-intellectualism of the official communist and socialist parties in France and Germany. But, for whatever reason, the divorce between the left intelligentsia and the masses had become an accomplished fact in most Western countries by the mid-1950s. This gave rise to a specific form of consciousness among left intellectuals. A writer for *Nezavisimaya Gazeta*, which in the 1990s became the mouthpiece of Moscow intellectuals, noted ironically:

In Paris in the 1950s people believed devoutly in the method of criticism and in its cleansing power. In empirical terms a critic might not differ in any way from a bourgeois; the main thing was that the critic should maintain a reflexive distance between himself or herself and the bourgeoisie. The pleasure which the left intellectual derived from criticizing the bourgeoisie had its equivalent at the opposite pole in the masochist pleasure which the bourgeoisie itself felt at each new round of sensational revelations. Like a sponge, capitalism soaked up and turned to its own use any criticism, however revolutionary in its intent. Meanwhile revolutionary excesses were successfully exported beyond Europe, to countries for which this criticism had not originally been meant at all.[3]

Intellectuals have a natural desire to be radical; this is how they prove their superiority over the 'grey' masses, whether these masses are bourgeois, proletarian or consumerist. The desire is inherent in intellectuals to show that they see more and look further than the average philistine – or, in other words, to prove their right to be considered intellectuals. No less natural is the human longing for a comfortable existence within the framework of the system – the system on which research funding, academic posts and publication in prestigious journals might well depend. Reconciling these needs has always been difficult, but never before has it been a problem of political theory.

It is enough to read the book by Anthony Giddens *Beyond Left and Right* to appreciate that the new radicalism which arose early in the 1990s in Western academic circles, and that by the middle of the decade had taken hold of masses of disappointed professors, provided a marvellous solution to this quandary. The final defeat of socialism, which to Giddens appears self-evident, simply wipes the struggle for systemic change off the agenda. In its place we are offered a set of slogans, ideas and approaches capable of brightening the lives of bored Western philistines in the epoch after the end of history.

These slogans, of course, call above all else for a broadening of democracy, and not only for a broadening, but for a qualitative improvement in line with the latest demands of academic sociology:

> Dialogic democracy is not centred on the state, but, as I shall argue, refers back on it in an important way. Situated in the context of globalization and social reflexivity, dialogic democracy encourages the *democratizing of democracy* within the sphere of the liberal democratic polity.[4]

Everything is simple and clear, is it not?

The next points in the programme will be a revival of community spirit, efforts to 'repair damaged solidarities' and, finally, of course, 'life politics'. For anyone who has not understood, the British sociologist explains his point more exactly: 'Life politics is a politics, not of *life chances*, but of *life style*.'[5]

Dialogue, communities, solidarities – all this is really very heartening, and warms the soul. But questions remain. For example: whose solidarities, and which communities? What kind of dialogue, between whom and, most importantly, about what? Dialogue *as a minimum* requires a common language, and a common interest as well.

When communities become consolidated, the process very often is not spontaneous, but is aimed at furthering the struggle against other communities. A community of cannibals might cultivate touching relations of mutual assistance among its members, but this does not seem so idyllic from the point of view of the people on whom the community feasts. Solidarity is most often necessary for defence against a common enemy, or for attacks on this enemy. And who is this enemy. As they say in Russia, 'Who are we going to be friends against, comrades?'

The politics urged by the British professor does not touch on structures or on systemic factors (the very concept of 'structure' is scarcely encountered in this sociology). Giddens, of course, takes meticulous account of the existence of capitalism and of the problems of inequality. The trouble is that he considers 'radical democratization' in isolation, and capitalism and inequality in isolation as well. Otherwise 'democratic dialogue', from being fond family conversation, might turn into a row with smashed crockery and broken heads. In the field of radical democracy, prosperous bourgeois will find self-fulfilment in discussing questions of mutual interest with other such individuals. For oppressed people and countries the British professor has his own recommendation, which will make it possible to resolve all problems amicably: the need is for 'lifestyle pacts, particularly one between the affluent and the poor'.[6] A true British gentleman, Giddens is prepared to let barbarians from Eastern Europe and the Third World live according to their own 'alternative' rules and traditions (the latter on a selective basis) so long as this does not affect his own way of life or his prosperity, which is founded on the superexploitation of these barbarians and the use of their resources. 'A positive move towards a post-scarcity system on the part of the global consumer class, coupled to an "alternative development" for the world's poor, are the only plausible means of creating a more equal world.'[7] If the sociologist does not know of other means, that proves such means cannot exist.

Unfortunately, the radical professor's noble intentions cannot be put into effect. In the first place, 'alternative development', if it is meant seriously, must remove resources and labour power from the sphere of capitalist exploitation; only if this is done can it be termed 'alternative' and not complementary. Second, the 'global consumer' is a pure sociological fiction that could arise only in the brain of an academic researcher. It is something like the average temperature of the patients in a hospital ward. Despite the global standardization of consumption, there is not just one consumption standard in the world, but several, reflecting not only such factors as cultural and climatic differences, but also the stratification of capitalist society itself. And since alternative development and a more just distribution of resources (including between economic sectors in Western countries themselves) cannot fail to affect the existing order, the question inevitably arises: who is going to pay for all this? Will a rise in living standards in developing countries be compensated by a decrease in wages in the Old World? (It should be noted that British workers in the mid-1990s already earned less than those in South Korea.) Or should the elites sacrifice something?

As soon as such questions start to be asked, mild gentlemanly dialogue somehow keeps being replaced by the harsh class demands that, according to Giddens, are vanishing into the past. The circuit has been closed.

It is not hard to see that, despite all the new terminology, what is before us is no more than a repeat edition, a re-make, of the bourgeois radicalism of the nineteenth century, which combined concern for the position of the poor, the demand for the broadening of democracy, and the cultural self-assertion of the members of the 'middle class' with a simultaneous refusal to pose the question of systemic changes and class solidarity. Repetition of the past is a natural phenomenon for an epoch of reaction. The problem, however, lies in the fact that the present repeat edition is noticeably inferior. The old radicalism paved the way for socialism; even if its protests were inconsistent, it was full of sincere enthusiasm in making them. Its cultural traditions found their continuation in communism, anarchism and modernist art. The present liberal (or 'post-socialist') radicalism is splenetic in tone; it contains neither enthusiasm, nor heroism, nor despair, nor protest.

Discursive Struggles

No one can accuse the 1990s-style radicals of supporting traditional bourgeois values. There is no longer any need for them to do so. Symbolic, ritual protest against 'traditional bourgeois values' has become a market symbol in itself. It can be bought and sold. Tom Frank, the editor of the Chicago journal *The Buffler*, notes that the modern market needs cultural diversity just as it needs new goods.

> The countercultural idea has become capitalist orthodoxy, its hunger for transgression upon transgression, change for the sake of change, now perfectly suited to an economic-cultural regime that runs on ever-faster cyclings of the new; its taste for self-fulfillment and its intolerance for the confines of tradition now permitting vast latitude in consuming practices and lifestyle experimentation. For consumerism is no longer about 'conformity' but about 'difference'. Advertising teaches us not in the ways of puritanical self-denial (a bizarre notion on the face of it), but in orgiastic, never-ending self-fulfillment. It counsels not rigid adherence to the tastes of the herd but vigilant and constantly-updated individualism. We consume not to fit in but to prove, on the surface at least, that we are rock'n'roll rebels, each of us as rule-breaking and hierarchy-defying as our heroes of the 60s, who now pitch cars, shoes and beer.[8]

In Eastern Europe this link between consumer capitalism, individualism and counter-cultural youth revolt has been even more obvious, since even in the 1960s this revolt was never aimed directly against capitalism. Western institutions arrived together with rock music, Coca-Cola together with feminism, and neo-liberalism together with pacifism, strange hairdos and free love. Anti-war protest went together easily with the acceptance of Western values, since it was necessary to liquidate the national armies which had earlier threatened these values. Western capitalism had its own traditions, while Eastern European neo-liberalism represented the negation of the traditions of communism. Its ideology was simple, limited and attractive: money opens the way to a world of diversity, self-realization and freedom.

The legalization of homosexuality in Russia coincided with the beginning of the transition to capitalism. Gay activism as a distinct movement did not exist here; if a certain politicization of homosexuals had taken place, this was exclusively within the framework of right-wing neo-liberal ideology. This shows how naive was the readiness of Western leftists to see 'natural' allies in any minority movements. The ending of discrimination against minorities is a general democratic demand, and it must be supported. But it can be organically linked to the programme of the left only in the degree to which the oppression of a particular minority is a necessary condition for the reproduction of capital.

Capitalism, Tom Frank notes, has changed more than the conception which the left has of it.

> Capitalism has changed dramatically since the 1950s, but our understanding of how it is to be resisted hasn't budged. As existential rebellion has become the more or less official style of Information Age capitalism, so has the countercultural notion of a static, repressive Establishment grown hopelessly obsolete. However the basic impulses of the countercultural idea may (and that's a big 'may') have disturbed a nation lost in Cold War darkness, they are today in fundamental agreement with the basic tenets of Information Age business theory. So close are they, in fact, that it has become impossible to understand the countercultural idea as anything more than the self-justifying ideology of the new dominant class that has arisen since the 1960s, the cultural means by which this group has proven itself ever so much better skilled than its slow-moving, security-minded forebears at adapting to the accelerated, always-changing consumerism of today. The anointed cultural opponents of capitalism are now capitalism's ideologues.[9]

The gap between criticism and action might not seem as painful as in the 1950s, when intellectuals themselves were not yet fully conscious of it. In the turbulent days of the 1960s criticism itself seemed to constitute a challenge to the existing order. But the decline of the left movement, caused among other factors by the chronic gap between theory and practice, thought and action, led ultimately to the degeneration of intellectual criticism as well. In general, struggling with bourgeois morality made sense only in that blessed time when the bourgeoisie itself had a certain morality and certain principles apart from extracting profit at any cost.

Theories are becoming more and more subtle, and more and more intellectually demanding. But they are addressed not to society, or at the masses, or even the identity groups to which they are formally dedicated, but only to a narrow circle of producers and consumers of ideology. The 'word games' are becoming increasingly elitist. The bearers of the new ideas are already isolating themselves not only from the mass movement, but also from the significant sector of the intelligentsia that is perturbed by the crisis of education, the erosion of traditional democratic values and the deterioration of its own position in society. A combination of politically correct language and academic jargon acts as a sort of code for the initiated, preventing the articulation of simple human feelings and needs, of clear and concrete demands. The authors of the detailed and thorough *Encyclopedia of the American Left* were even forced to devote several paragraphs to clarifying 'often-confusing Left terminology' for the benefit of readers.[10] This was in an encyclopedia meant for specialists.

For postmodernist theoreticians revolution, just like reform, is no more than 'narrative'. But revolution and reform amount in practical terms to the life experience of millions of people – tragic, painful and disillusioning perhaps, but absolutely real, and having nothing in common with various 'narratives' or 'discourses'.

Fredric Jameson accurately described the polemic by the postmodernist left against the old Marxism as a discursive struggle. As Jameson remarks, 'everything in our social life – from economic value and state power to practices and to the very structure of the psyche itself – can be said to have become "cultural" in some original and as yet untheorized sense'.[11] This creates the possibility of discursive struggle when images and verbal associations effectively replace arguments. It is enough to attach positive or negative associations to particular words; by simply employing these words, you can then 'prove' whatever you like. 'Good' words are 'grass-roots', 'local', 'community', 'civil society', 'association' and so forth; 'bad' words are 'state', 'centralization' and 'control'. It matters nothing what might lie behind these words. To explain, for example, that some technological processes create a need for centralization, while others are incompatible with it, is as useless as trying to discuss music with the deaf.

Postmodernist Marxism has promised to go 'beyond the totalizing notions of capitalism and class struggle that characterize classical Marxism'. The political result of this operation is to be 'a new kind of class struggle' meant to 'take into account the meaning of everyday activities as we demystify and contextualize grand narratives of revolution'.[12]

When it rejects 'totalization' in the name of the concrete, postmodernism is in its own way correct. Not because all 'totalization' is totalitarian (this is no more than a play on words, possible only in Western languages). The point is simply that any generalization can be broken down to the point where it loses all meaning. We might join with Margaret Thatcher and declare that society does not exist; that there are only institutions, groups and families. But these do not exist either, since in reality there are only individual people. For that matter, people do not exist either, since they consist only of cells, molecules, atoms and so forth. The same intellectual operation can be performed in the opposite direction, proving that nothing exists except society. In reality, of course, all these phenomena exist, since they are all equally real and equally concrete. But these truths, that are quite obvious to ordinary people, are by no means so obvious to intellectuals.

The enthusiasm of the postmodernist left for 'anti-totalization', despite being a figment of intellectuals' thought processes, is anti-intellectual in its basic character. The struggle against 'totalization' is in reality a struggle against scientific thought and, ultimately, against thought as such. A complete and final liberation of the intellectual makes him or her quite independent of the object of thought, of his or her own conclusions, and of the process itself. Thought in the old sense is replaced by speech, by discourse, by the associating of words.

For academic radicals, real political struggle has always been something alien, consisting at best of vicarious experiencing of the exploits and tragedies of others through the medium of 'solidarity campaigns'. Cynthia Kaufman laments that following the defeat of the revolutions in Nicaragua and El Salvador, which was followed by the collapse of the Soviet bloc:

> this whole dream, which sustained and nurtured the oppositional imagination of much of the anticapitalist US Left collapsed. Without it, anticapitalist work has been hard to sustain. Indeed, it is even difficult to say what we mean by anticapitalist work anymore.[13]

However, 'solidarity campaigns' have never been 'anticapitalist'. In themselves they have not undermined the bases of the system. Recalling the unsuccessful campaign by the left against the North American Free Trade Agreement (NAFTA), Kaufman concludes with the words: 'What a difference it would have made if we had been working with a labor movement full of grassroots organizers, well trained and rooted in their communities. We probably would have won that battle.'[14] But who would have won in such a case? Intellectuals with their 'narratives' and 'discourses', or trade union activists, for whom political work was a habitual and at times painful aspect of daily life?

Theory has a certain point only if it interprets and reinterprets concrete practice, instead of various 'narratives'. Postmodernist Marxism has had no relationship to the changes that have occurred in the American trade unions. However, the prolonged and little-rewarded work of radical groups such as, say, Labor Notes has had a bearing on these changes. While some people have theorized about the meaning of 'anticapitalist work' and have tried to 're-imagine capitalism', others have struggled against capitalism in practice.

In the new system of reference points the ideological place of the proletariat, taking on itself the world-historic mission of liberating humanity, is occupied by oppressed groups and minorities – racial, religious, national and sexual. All are of equal worth and significance, and no one can claim a 'leading' or 'historic' role. Nevertheless, women have a special place in the hierarchy of 'minorities', though strictly speaking they are a majority.

Feminism: from Protest to Career Politics

The politics of feminism comes closest of all to matching the criteria of postmodernist ideology. In the 1970s and 1980s feminism was on the rise. 'The very success of the movement to date means that these forces speak with more authority from their institutional positions in academia, the state bureaucracy, parliament, the legal arena and, to a lesser degree, the corporate boardroom', writes the Australian journalist Pat Brewer. 'This legitimises their "feminism" while drowning out other views.'[15] However, political success is as transient as fashion, especially if it is not consolidated through structural changes in society. The gains of feminism were placed in question by the neo-conservative wave of the 1990s.

By no means all women have been inclined to share the fundamental thesis of radical feminism concerning the need to struggle against 'patriarchal' society, 'in which women as a group are oppressed and exploited by men as a group'.[16] Nor have the ideas of 'freedom' and 'self-affirmation' propagandized by feminist ideologues been greeted with enthusiasm in all cultures. Most importantly, by no means all women who suffer from discrimination have been willing to embrace the strategies and ideologies of the representatives of the Western middle class who have expressed their worldview in radical feminism.

In the early 1990s, when the ideas of American feminism began to be widely disseminated in Russia, *Nezavisimaya Gazeta* published an article by Irina Glushchenko entitled 'Women's Happiness'. Here it was observed that a profound difference existed between the historical women's movement of the nineteenth and early twentieth centuries and Western feminism in the form which it had assumed by the 1970s. It is significant that the Western feminism that was imported into the countries of the former Soviet bloc had no links with the revolutionary tradition of the Russian women's movement of the early twentieth century, represented for example in the views and activity of Aleksandra Kollontay.

In the narrow sense, the programme of the emancipation of women was fulfilled with the winning of legal equality in most Western countries (in many countries the introduction of women's suffrage coincided with the abolition of other restrictions on voting rights, such as property and religious qualifications). But this did not guarantee real equality of opportunity. For this reason the women's movement of the 1920s was closely linked to the labour movement: it sought to improve the position of women by changing society. 'However strange it might seem, feminism arose to a significant degree from the dissatisfaction felt by middle- and upper-class women with the existing women's movement.'[17] Feminist ideologues themselves recognize that there is a fundamental difference between their positions and the historical women's movement, which they describe as 'old feminism'.[18] To express both the continuity and the difference, they use the term 'new feminism' or 'second-wave feminism'. Earlier, the central idea was equality; now it is identity. In Glushchenko's view, however, this difference is so fundamental that we are faced with two quite different movements, aimed at achieving quite distinct goals that are often opposed to one another.

As soon as the talk ceases to be about feminism, but about feminists, the feminist 'identity' turns out to be an ambiguous and disorienting political slogan. On the one hand it is imaginary, while to the degree that it is nevertheless real it acts as a tool of liberal hegemony in the women's movement, subjugating leftists to the tasks and objectives of the right.

The laudable effort made by leftists to assimilate the feminist critique of old-style socialism and to rethink their own approaches has led ultimately to an uncritical borrowing of the ideology and slogans of the liberal women's movement. 'The left is feminist or it is not the left', declared the participants in a women's conference of the Party of Democratic Socialism in Germany.[19] What does this mean? If it means that the old socialism, oriented exclusively to the values and ideas of men, can no longer satisfy millions of working women, one can only agree. If it signifies a rejection of the old communist practice in which women's associations and other 'specialized' formations were no more than front organizations for the party, which ran them on the principle of 'transmission belts', then it is quite correct. But if it means sharing the tasks and goals of right-wing liberal groups acting under the banner of feminism, it is a call to capitulation.

Despite pointing out the differences between left and right in the feminist movement, socialist ideologues try to evade the question of the class significance of these contradictions. As a result they finish up in a schizophrenic situation. While acknowledging that a section of the feminist movement puts forward ideas, demands and slogans with which it is impossible to agree, they call at the same time for solidarity with these groups.

The trouble is that the common, that is, extra-social interests of women (just like the notorious 'universal human values') either lie outside of politics, or will become an appropriate topic for the political process in post-capitalist society, when today's social contradictions have in one degree or another been resolved.

If the rise of the old women's movement was closely linked to the general rise of the democratic and socialist movements, the flourishing of the 'new feminism' is linked to their decline. Tens of thousands of young people from prosperous families were politicized and radicalized by the events of the 1960s, but this did not last for long. The 'new left' developed in isolation from the traditional labour movement. The point is not just that the workers proved to be more moderate in their views, but as Donald Sassoon notes, that the radicalization of the students occurred against a background of the de-politicization of workers. Even inside the 'old' socialist parties the worker was no longer the central figure.

> Fewer workers were now participating in traditional socialist politics, but nor were they joining any of the new organizations and movements. It appeared that politics was becoming a more middle-class affair, though it was important to remember that the middle class was now large, not the small elite it was at the beginning of the century.[20]

This was an alarming symptom, a sign of an impending crisis of democracy and of a ripening contradiction between civil society and society as it actually was. But amid the fever of the turbulent 1960s it went unnoticed.

With the defeat of the 'new left', the political culture of the middle class began to change. For many of the participants in student protests, this meant rejecting radicalism.

> Feminism was born out of the decay of the new left. The women who came to feminism did so as a rule for two reasons. For some it represented a way out of radical politics,

while for others it had the reverse function, allowing them to remain politically active at a time when the left movement was in crisis.[21]

The rise of the feminist movement in the West was greeted by the left with sincere enthusiasm. 'In country after country, women have taken part in large-scale campaigns against reactionary abortion and contraceptive statutes, oppressive marriage laws, inadequate childcare facilities and legal restrictions on equality', wrote the authors of a pamphlet published in Australia under the editorship of Pat Brewer:

> They have exposed and resisted the myriad ways in which sexism is expressed in all spheres – from politics, employment and education to the most intimate aspects of daily life, including the weight of domestic drudgery and the violence and intimidation that women are subjected to in the home and the street.
> This new radicalisation of women has been unprecedented in the depth of the economic, social, ideological and political ferment it expresses and in its implications for the struggle against capitalist oppression and exploitation.[22]

Left-wing writers in the mid-1990s viewed the situation in the women's movement far more sceptically. However, the need to go 'beyond the fragments' was already clear in the late 1970s, when the political and ideological heterogeneity of the social movements was not yet so obvious. Hilary Wainwright wrote, in 1979:

> If workers were simply up against bosses, women up against the sexual division of labour and sexist culture, blacks against racial oppression and discrimination, with no significant connection between these forms of oppression, no state power linking and overseeing the institutions concerned, then strong independent movements would be enough. But it is precisely the connections between these sources of oppression, both through the state and through the organization of production and culture, which makes such a piecemeal solution impossible.[23]

The complicating factor is that in reality partial solutions are indeed possible, since the problems of some oppressed groups can often be solved at the expense of others.

The mass feminist movement changed the relationship of forces in society, and undoubtedly had an emancipatory potential. It was capable only of serving as the first stage for a more profound politicization of women. The pragmatic Donald Sassoon notes: 'From the perspective of socialism, feminism presented a challenge and an opportunity: to break the dominance of conservative ideas among the majority of women.'[24] However, a genuine radicalization would have been possible only if the women who were being drawn into politics had felt themselves to be equally representatives of their class. The spirit of feminism, by contrast, was directed against class ideology. As a result, the spread of feminist ideas did not by any means weaken the influence of political conservatism among women. The feminist slogans that were included in the programmes of all left parties, from the most moderate to the most radical, had only an insignificant effect on the behaviour of women voters. As a British historian states:

> It is not evident that the adoption of feminist (or ecological) positions benefited the parties of the Left electorally though it is unlikely to have damaged any of them. Women like men have multiple identities and are not necessarily swayed by feminist arguments. In most countries, class, education, religion and regions are better predictions of voting behaviour than sex. The idea that the mere adoption of a set of demands would automatically detach a definite portion of the electorate was a fantasy, held only by those who could not tell the difference between a market of commodities and the political market.[25]

The idea that political life does not operate according to the laws of the market remains beyond even many left-wing intellectuals.

Individualist Mass Movements

Against the background of the overall crisis of left politics in the 1980s and 1990s, the problems arising out of the new social movements have not only gone unsolved, but have become much more profound. Although it is socialists who have been most persistent in defending the rights of minorities and the interests of women, it is by no means true that the real shifts here have always involved a turn to the left. The situation has been similar with the environmental movement, which in the early 1980s was regarded as a new, post-industrial form of anti-capitalist opposition. As Sassoon notes:

> the essence of the 'green' idea was that it was necessary to regulate and constrain capitalist firms in order to impose some general – hence 'collectivist' – goals, such as a better environment. Ideologically, this was far more acceptable to the Left than to the Right.[26]

The real environmental movement, however, has not made a rapprochement with socialism but, on the contrary, has moved further and further away from it. The cause has been the weakness of the left parties themselves; these have sought less to rethink socialism through the prism of environmental ideas than to hide themselves from these ideas. Just as bankrupt have been the claims of environmental movements to stand 'above the traditional division into right and left'. The claims that the destruction of the environment affects rich and poor alike have merely testified to the unwillingness of environmentalist leaders seriously to confront the question of the structural causes of the environmental crisis, of the relationship between the destruction of nature and the economic logic of capitalism. The desire of many environmentalists to evade the question of capitalism and socialism has simply created political problems inside the movement. By the late 1990s the flimsiness of 'Green' ideology had become impossible to hide. As Norberto Bobbio has rightly observed, it is becoming more and more obvious 'that the spread of ecological movements will not make the traditional left/right split anachronistic, but that instead, this split will be reproduced within the various ecological movements, which are already troubled by internal divisions, despite their recent appearance'.[27]

It is now difficult to find a party which calls openly for discrimination against women and for the destruction of nature; in this sense the ideas of feminism and environmentalism have really become hegemonic. Nevertheless, the destruction of nature continues, while the position of the majority of women has either failed to improve or has even deteriorated. On the level of slogans it has been easy for bourgeois parties to seize the initiative, since many of the demands raised have been perfectly compatible with their own ideology. 'While liberal parties have paid the most lip service to issues specifically affecting women, the feminist ideas and concerns have also had an impact on the most conservative parties', notes Pat Brewer.[28] 'Many of the values of the new social movements could easily be co-opted by most parties, not just those of the left', observes Sassoon:

> By the end of the twentieth century, no conservative or liberal party would oppose the idea that women and men should have equal rights, or that the environment should be protected, or that minorities should be safeguarded. Conservative voters in rural or suburban districts frequently oppose the construction of an airport or a motorway by using the themes, even the methods, of green activists.[29]

The right of women to hold jobs outside the home has become the topic of heated discussions within the Australian National Party. The left wing of the Liberal Party, which later split off to form the Australian Democrats, has chosen women to lead its parliamentary fraction and has supported the demands of the feminist movement. 'However, when it comes to social programmes that would have immediate and significant economic impact – such as the expansion of cheap, high standard, child-care facilities – the gains made by women have been virtually non-existent.'[30] In other words, there is a fundamental gap between the readily fulfilled demands of the liberal 'new feminism' and the interests of the majority of working women. Irina Glushchenko writes:

> Arising as a reaction to the individualism of Western society, feminism in its way is a reflection of this individualism. The main criticism which feminists make is directed against the 'patriarchal order', but in a genuine patriarchal society feminism is impossible. The social actors in patriarchal society are not individuals, but families, clans, local communities and the state. The heads of families, clans or states are as a rule men. But this does not mean that men rule over women. The overwhelming majority of men and women alike are subordi-

nated alike to the collective. Furthermore, they are incapable as a rule of imagining themselves outside of the collective, or of acting outside the framework of the general interest and of the general culture or customary law.

Consequently, it is quite incorrect to portray patriarchal society in terms of 'the power of men'. Moreover, all patriarchal societies retain quite strongly developed matriarchal elements. The more backward and patriarchal a society, the more matriarchal features are to be found within it. Thus in China, the main figure in the family is traditionally the grandmother. Women are certainly forced to perform housework, but they also have full control over everything concerned with this sphere of life. Moreover, in large matriarchal families older women exercise control not only over younger women, but also over the younger women's husbands. Ask any Russian man about the role which his mother-in-law plays in his life! In modern Western society, by contrast, the status of mother-in-law is to a large degree merely formal.

Feminism ignores these aspects of life, reducing everything to a mechanistic opposition between women and men, instead of recognizing the complex issues of family hierarchies.

In Soviet society it was difficult to speak of male authority, since in most cases women played the major role in the family. Among Westerners, the lack of self-sufficiency of our men was the topic of frequent jokes. As a rule, a woman took all her husband's wages, and each day gave him back as much as she considered he needed. In the family, husbands were treated as children who needed to have everything decided for them. It is well known that a wife was likely to write a letter to the party committee in the enterprise where her husband worked if he was unfaithful to her, drank or in general behaved badly. Such a letter could easily ruin a man's career.

The problems of the patriarchal family are simply incomprehensible in the West, where the nuclear family has long since triumphed. Nuclear families also exist outside the West, but as a rule, only in the first or second generation. In poorer countries nuclear families may well be unviable – in the absence of the extended family, a married couple often cannot feed themselves.

The presence of a combination of patriarchy and matriarchy, such as existed in Soviet society, means that phrases about male domination mean nothing in themselves. Patriarchal society is based on a system of mutual obligations. This system is not symmetrical, and its destruction often affects women more painfully than men. But in certain respects, it subjects men to very strict rules.

In bourgeois society private individuals are not bound by any obligations apart from formal legal ones. Their personal relationships as well are merely formal, or are based on mutual agreement. Everyone is free, and each must look out for himself or herself. However, a normal society cannot exist in such circumstances; the family, and ties with relatives, must be retained despite the triumph of individualism. In practice, bourgeois individualism has freed only men, reducing to a minimum their obligations toward family and kin.

For women, individualism has turned out to be an unattainable luxury. We thus encounter a contradiction, in that the more developed the society, the more women have sought to partake of individualism, freeing themselves from traditional obligations.

In the early years of the century what was involved was formal achievements: the right to hold a job and to vote in elections. Now, the question concerns the ability of women to share in a general way in the values and rights of individualism. But if this occurred on a broad scale, society could simply not survive. Obviously, the demands for equal rights bear witness to the crisis of the existing social order. But if these demands were fulfilled, the crisis would not be solved, but would become still deeper.

Meanwhile, such demands have no point in a real patriarchal society, where collectivist relations have not yet been undermined by individualism. This is the reason behind the initially puzzling phenomenon of women from the most 'backward' countries, who appear to be subject to heavy oppression, proving totally unreceptive to the calls of Western activists who dream of 'liberating' them. It also explains why the ideas of feminism are alien to many women in Russia.

One of the reasons for the rise of feminism is that men lead an individualist way of life, and women a patriarchal one. In the West, the calls to liberate women from the patriarchal order and to render them equal to men in all respects amount to one and the same thing. But beyond the borders of the West, in societies where the patriarchal order is general for all, the one does not follow from the other.[31]

Hence Western feminism, in Glushchenko's view, has not only absorbed the ideology of 'alienated individualism', but has also broken decisively with the traditions of the earlier women's movement. From struggling to change society, it has moved on to trying to bring about the more effective participation of women in the existing system, restructuring and modernizing the social elites. This feminism is not simply reformist, but bourgeois; it expresses the needs of women of the upper and middle classes. The result of this is a growing dissatisfaction with feminism not only in the lower orders of society, but also among women who belong to the working middle layers. An example of this dissatisfaction is Rene Denfeld's book *The New Victorians*, which shows how the hostility to male sexuality cultivated by radical feminism has a good deal in common with puritan-Victorian repressive bourgeois morality. In Denfeld's view, 'real feminism' implants in most women the psychology of the approving onlooker, and not of the activist. As a result the new generation – the 'daughters of feminism' – is leaving the women's movement.[32] The growth of repressiveness in the political practice of feminism is also noted by Lynne Segal. In particular, the campaign against pornography 'is opening up the threat of quite unprecedented levels of censorship through harassing law suits and financial penalties against producers, distributors, booksellers, writers, photographers and movie makers'.[33] As the positions of radical feminism have become more harsh, the original liberating content of the women's movement has been driven out. Those leftists who have become the willing hostages of this ideology have finished up in a moral dead-end.

Moving East

During the 1990s postmodernist radicalism has been actively exported not only to Eastern Europe, but also to the countries of the Third World. As a new Western fashion, it has received active support among local left elites. For example, postmodernism was declared the theme of the 1996 Calcutta Book Fair, organized by the communist government of West Bengal. This could not fail to have an impact on the political culture of the left. In India even serious radical women activists, educated in the spirit of Western feminism, 'were reluctant to have discussions with, or relate to, the masses of urban poor, peasant and working class women . . . they felt that they were so different and that couldn't fight together because they wouldn't be "appropriating their issues"'.[34] The Turkish supporter of socialist feminism Meltem Ahiska notes that, despite all efforts, it has not been possible to overcome 'the gap between feminists and other women'.[35] This contradiction effectively reproduces the division of society into a Westernized minority (in Turkey, very significant) and a traditional majority.

In cases where the women's movement has arisen spontaneously 'from below', the feminist 'elite' has not been ready for this, and has remained on the sidelines. This was the case during the Zapatista revolt in Mexico. 'The initiatives of the Zapatista women have outstripped the feminist movement just as they have outstripped the left', states the Paris journal *Inprecor*. 'Their demands seem very simple, but they are fundamental.'[36] The Zapatista women merely demanded the right to choose their husbands themselves, and to take part in political life – rights which bourgeois women won almost a hundred years ago. But this movement, which challenged patriarchal traditions, was not the result of feminist propaganda. It arose out of the needs of the oppressed – out of demands by women, and by men as well, that their human dignity be respected.

According to the ideologues of feminism, women in 'backward' countries are so oppressed and downtrodden that they cannot even speak out in defence of their rights. The oppression of women in most of these countries is beyond question, but the remedies prescribed by feminism are by no means so indisputable. The ideology of Western feminism contradicts a traditional culture which is also an important token of identity for most of the population, including women. The traditional culture is under pressure from Western 'cultural imperialism', and its decay is closely linked with the strengthening of the hegemony of transnational corporations. Meanwhile, mainstream feminism is characterized by the same orientation toward the values of Western culture, the values which must supposedly be asserted among 'backward' peoples.

The transformation of the Western (or Westernized) woman into a cultural norm clearly represents a dead-end. It is essential to recognize that the specific concepts, methods and values of feminism themselves bear the stamp of social and cultural narrow-mindedness. An anecdotal example of the mutual incomprehension which prevails between Westernized adherents of middle-class feminism and the mass of working women in non-Western countries is provided by the response when the Indian literary theorist Gayatari Chakravorty Spivak gave a lecture to a group of village women. Hearing her post-modernist terminology, 'the audience became very angry and asked her how it was relevant to their lives. When she couldn't answer, they asked her to translate her paper into Bengali, which of course she couldn't!'[37]

Although bourgeois women and women from the oppressed layers of society both encounter discrimination, they often encounter discrimination of a quite different kind. Miliband notes that 'they do not suffer in the same manner'.[38] The problem, however, goes deeper. The discrimination against bourgeois women is not class-based, and is indeed aimed at maintaining, in pure form, the power of men within the elite. The discrimination against working women, by contrast, is often simply a means of ensuring the additional exploitation of cheap labour power (just as the labour of immigrants, for example, is exploited). In the first case counterposing men to women appears logical, but in the second it merely impedes the development of the solidarity that is essential if the problems of the oppressed are to be solved.

The Real Differences

Traditional Marxism has been dominated by the idea of the uniformity imposed by the capitalist factory. But in fact, various types of organization and cultures of production have coexisted even within the framework of the industrial economy. The Russian socialist movement encountered this phenomenon early in the century when the Jewish workers' union, the *Bund*, made its appearance. This was one of the first left-wing organizations to be constructed not on a territorial but on an ethnic basis. The Bund arose earlier than the All-Russian Social Democratic Party and served as its prototype (it was no accident that many activists of the Bund later played important roles in the Menshevik Party). The Jewish workers' organization had its own distinctive features. While Russian and Ukrainian workers were concentrated in big plants, Jewish workers predominated in small workshops of a semi-artisan type. The combination of ethnic with class solidarity made possible the rapid organization of a party, but the Bund later ran up against severe problems. It could not achieve its goals outside the broader social democratic movement, but within this movement it sought constantly to affirm its separate identity as 'the sole representative of the Jewish proletariat'.[39] The Bund became the topic of bitter disputes, and at the Second Congress of the Russian Social Democratic Workers Party the debate 'on the place of the Bund within the party' boiled over into the split between the Bolsheviks and Mensheviks.

Ethnic divisions of labour are a reality of capitalism. Wallerstein writes:

> There seem to be various advantages to the ethnicization of occupational categories. Different kinds of relations of production, we may assume, require different kinds of normal behaviour by the work force. Since this behaviour is not in fact genetically determined, it must be taught. Work forces need to be socialized into reasonably specific sets of attitudes. The 'culture' of an ethnic group is precisely the set of rules into which parents belonging to that ethnic group are pressured to socialize their children. The state or the school system can do this of course. But they usually seek to avoid performing that particularistic function alone or too overtly, since it violates the concept of 'national' equality for them to do so.[40] States which divide people on the basis of their skin colour are condemned. The United States prides itself on having freed the slaves, and the apartheid system in South Africa collapsed as a result of pressure from the world community and of the resistance of black inhabitants who wanted merely to be citizens with the same rights as whites. But ethnic nationalism reproduces this same division from below, and on a voluntary basis. 'Thus what is illegitimate for the state to do comes in by the rear window as "voluntary" group behaviour defending a social "identity"'.[41]

In other words, the capitalist system reproduces different identities, and has a need for them. Their preservation, development and strengthening represent very important elements in the capitalist policies for reproducing labour power, for managing it and for maintaining control over it.[42] Identities are of course liable to change, but the economy changes as well. Socialist organizations that idealize and reproduce 'the discipline of the factory' have in many ways also helped to train labour power for capitalist production. But through affirming the principles of solidarity and mutual aid, they have at the same time issued a challenge to the system. Identity politics, on the other hand, helps to strengthen the existing situation. Despite its radical slogans, it is conservative and opportunist.

The proponents of identity politics are convinced that, in speaking out against the oppression of their particular group, they are acting in the interests of general emancipation. The oppression, however, is linked with division, which also reflects the identities that have been established. Politics that are aimed at crystallizing differences, and not at consolidating common interests, serve in practice to de-class hired workers. The objective position of workers in society does not in itself guarantee their class being. The alternative to class-based social practice may simply be the pointless seething of a 'proletarianized' and atomized mass that is incapable of political action. The politics of emancipation must be aimed at going beyond the bounds of identities. The goal should not be to suppress these identities mechanically (which is impossible, since people are different, as is their cultural and social experience), but to surmount them, achieving unity on a higher level where differences of sex, education and skin colour become immaterial or secondary.

Feminist labour sociology assigns primary significance to the problem of sexual harassment in the workplace. Accordingly, it gives priority to demands of a juridical and ideological character: introducing harsher punishments for the guilty, taking measures to defend the victims, and so forth. Meanwhile, feminists have shown far less interest in the problems of part-time workers, since these problems are not specifically 'women's' issues. The women who have provided feminism with its core activists and supporters have been well educated and in full-time employment. The broad masses of women, situated on a lower rung of the social hierarchy, have simply been outside the field of vision of this feminist elite. Among the bulk of the female population conservative ideas and values have continued to hold sway, since no others have been on offer (the ideology of feminism has simply not been assimilated, since it bears no relation to these women's everyday experience). In order for these masses of women to be mobilized and to struggle for their rights, what is needed is not to call on them to remember their identity as women (they too have such an identity, though it is a non-feminist one), but to suggest a clear strategy through which they can struggle for their rights as part-time workers. In particular, the need is for these women to be organized in trade unions and to win collective agreements and, ultimately, for them to attain equal rights with full-time workers.

By no means the least important aspect of the question is the need to support the public sector, since experience shows that the rights of workers receive more respect there than in the private sector. Also involved is the complex process of reconciling the interests of full-time and part-time workers. All this lies outside the areas of interest of most feminist ideologues.[43] At the same time as middle-class feminists show little interest in the women who clean the floors in the offices, sturdy males in the trade unions prefer to have dealings with people who are like themselves. Millions of working women are left to fend for themselves.

The historical problem of socialism consists in the fact that, while expressing the interests of the industrial working class, it has tried at the same time to be a movement defending the rights of all the oppressed. The theoretical basis for this was set out by Marx and Engels in *The Communist Manifesto*, where they speak of the proletariat as the most oppressed class, and therefore as capable of the most determined struggle against all forms of oppression and exploitation. This broad social mission of the left is one of the sources of its strength, and of its ability to unite around itself substantial numbers of people not only in the developed capitalist states, but also in the countries of the periphery. But this social mission is also the source of problems and contradictions. Ultimately, it is from this that the initial impulse for replacing class politics with identity politics arises.

The Marxist Approach

Trying to combine Marxist analysis with the concepts prevailing among Western radical intellectuals, André Brie writes of the need to 'liberate' from the rule of capital 'the diversity, heterogeneity and contradictory nature of modern societies and economies'.[44] Meanwhile, the heterogeneity of modern society does not exist in a vacuum. It emerged and became established within the framework of capitalism, and reflects the problems and contradictions of capitalism in exactly the same way as the 'diversity' of feudal or caste society reflected the corresponding forms of domination and oppression.

As long ago as the 1920s it was alleged that Marxism, through reducing social development to the struggle between classes, was ignoring the diversity of social and cultural life. Nikolai Bukharin in his prison manuscripts of 1937 tried to answer this criticism, declaring that the problem could not be reduced to the counterposing of 'diversity' and 'uniformity'. 'There are various *qualitative* diversities, various *types* of them, various *measures* of diversity, and various sorts of relationships that they can have with *unity*.'[45] Drawing a contrast between chaotic sounds and a symphony (it is curious that the same comparison figures in the *Prison Notebooks* of Antonio Gramsci), Bukharin declared: 'Capitalist diversity divides people.' In essence, he maintained, this was all 'a *debased diversity* signifying the *wretchedness* of the lives of millions of people, its extreme *monotony*'.[46]

Unlike Bukharin, Gramsci considered that the chaos of sounds that emerges while the orchestra is tuning up is essential if the symphony is to ring forth. The sounds in each case are the same; the question is how they are organized. Despite the oversimplified opposition (chaos versus symphony) that is characteristic of his thinking, Bukharin was right where the arguments of his opponents were concerned; diversity in itself is neither a boon for society nor part of its 'riches'.

Transforming a broad left movement into a totality of 'specific' movements does not guarantee even the support of the respective 'specific' groups, which are well able to find other means of self-organization and self-expression. What is needed is not a mechanical 'unification', but collaboration on the basis of a strategic initiative. Whatever we may think of spontaneity, someone has to take on the role of a vanguard. A strategic initiative does not mean returning to the Bolshevik concept of the vanguard party. What is involved is not mechanical leadership by 'specialized' movements and 'front organizations', but the creation of new opportunities and prospects which various groups and forces will address independently. This activity has the potential to set up a resonance in society; it stimulates self-organization and an escalation of demands, as in the 1905 revolution in Russia, where there were revolutionary parties but no vanguard.

As the contradictions of identity politics become more and more obvious, the need emerges for inter-group and inter-ethnic solidarity. Some writers therefore try to suggest a new, broader approach:

> We must find new room in our identity as people of color to include all other oppressed national minorities – Chicanos, Puerto Ricans, Asian/Pacific Americans, and other people of African descent. We must find the common ground we share with oppressed people who are not national minorities – working class people, the physically challenged, the homeless, the unemployed, and those Americans who suffer discrimination because they are lesbian or gay.[47]

However radical such appeals may sound, all they express is the contradictory nature and lack of prospects of identity politics. First, the identities here are in reality products of the imagination, or the result of some conscious agreement between political activists; they can be arbitrarily refashioned in order to include (and consequently, to exclude) particular categories of people. This means that the 'identities' of radical politics have little in common with the real identities that take shape in the course of history, and that change only very slowly under the impact of collective and personal experience. Second, even the call for a 'broad bloc' seems quite demagogic coming from the ideologues of 'identity politics'. Any bloc turns out to be a mechanical coalition of groups.

In principle, such coalitions can be neither durable nor effective. Much as it is necessary to defend the rights of oppressed groups, their problems are not of equal significance for society. Any serious strategy therefore presupposes that an attempt will be made to distinguish the main contradictions and general strategic tasks whose solving will open up the possibility of dealing with others as well. In other words, any strategy involves a hierarchy of goals. Contrary to the ideas of revolutionaries in the past, victory on one front does not automatically ensure victory on another. Hence, the emancipation of the workers does not yet in itself represent the solving of the 'woman question'. In this respect the feminist and postmodernist critique of old-style socialism is reasonable and just. But a hierarchy of goals is nevertheless essential, since without it transforming complex and closely interwoven structures will be impossible. A strategic hierarchy is constructed neither on the principle of taste, nor on that of a 'living queue'. Its basis can only be an understanding of the general logic and social hierarchy of capitalist society itself.

As soon as identity politics becomes the ideology of real instead of imaginary political action, problems arise. 'What kind of anticapitalist interventions and strategies would require a poor working-class gay/lesbian subject position?'[48] Or: 'As a Black woman I am always asked which comes first, being Black or being a woman?'[49] Such questions are scarcely possible within the framework of ordinary human logic. Can there really be contradictions between race and sex? Each of us has dozens and perhaps even hundreds of 'identities', which in their sum make up our personality.

Doug Henwood in *Left Business Observer* remarks that the thinking of Americans about race seems 'extremely confused'. Public opinion surveys have shown that a significant proportion of respondents simply cannot answer a question about their identity. 'When people were asked to volunteer a category instead of choosing from the list, responses included 'Christian', 'Mason', 'Black Muslim' and 'rebellious teenager'. But even that is not all. Looking at the results of the survey, Henwood could not refrain from an ironic comment:

> One message is that the language of many leftists isn't in common use. A bit over half of 'Hispanics', 58%, preferred that term; 12% liked Latino; and the balance (30%) preferred some other form or none at all. Almost two-thirds, 62%, of 'whites' liked the prevailing form; 17% Caucasian; 2%, European-American; 1% Anglo; and the rest (18%) something else or nothing in particular. Among 'blacks', 44% preferred the official term; 28%, African-American; 12%, Afro-American;

3%, Negro; 1% colored; and 12% liked something else or had no preference.[50]

Hegemony and Postmodernist Strategy

The most serious representatives of postmodernist radicalism recognize that the weak point of the social and cultural movements lies in their isolation from one another. Thus Chantal Mouffe writes:

> These struggles do not spontaneously converge, and in order to establish democratic equivalences a new 'common sense' is necessary, which would transform the identity of different groups so that the demands of each group could be articulated with those of others according to the principle of democratic equivalence. For it is not a matter of establishing a mere alliance between given interests but of actually modifying the very identity of these forces.

A unification of forces has to be reached on the basis of 'a hegemony of democratic values', and in such a way as to ensure 'an equivalence between these different struggles'.[51]

The problem, however, lies in the fact that a common democratic and 'civic' culture is not enough for unity; this culture can only be the result of joint struggle, not one of the preconditions for it. Meanwhile, the idea of the equal importance of all movements rules out the possibility of hegemony, since hegemony is above all a system of priorities that is assimilated by the broad masses of people. This does not mean denying that 'secondary' demands are valuable in themselves. It merely signifies an understanding that unless the 'central' elements of the common programme are brought to fruition, the rest will not be realized anyway.

For Chantal Mouffe integration of different struggles does not require the formulation of strategic priorities. It has nothing to do with the class struggles or even with the experience of the people and their culture. It is a purely mechanistic process based on the general acceptance by everyone of some 'radical democratic' values formulated by the postmodernist intellectuals. In that sense her approach is also deeply authoritarian, though the author does not realize that.

The main problem with this kind of 'democratic equivalence' is that it simply will not work. Capitalism is structured hierarchically as a society and as an economic system. And because of that some forms of oppression and domination are *objectively* more important for the reproduction of the bourgeois order than others. Some relations are essential for capitalism, others are not, some compose the core of the system, others its periphery. And because of that, different struggles simply *cannot* be strategically equal whether we like it or not.

Marxists view the contradiction between labour and capital as the central one, both for the reproduction of the system and for the emancipation struggle. This does not mean, of course, that these struggles are not just. For those who suffer they may be much more important than other struggles waged to transform the world. But effective strategic unity can not be achieved without formulating priorities. The truth of the matter is precisely that different interests and identities can't be integrated mechanically and democratic equivalence at best will leave them coexisting peacefully, not converging. On the other hand, secondary interests cannot be simply subordinated to the primary ones. This is just another mechanistic approach and, as the experience of the vaguardist parties shows, it will not work either.

Will socialism resolve all contradictions and solve all problems we are facing under capitalism? Clearly, not. That is why many of the struggles will continue long after the victory of socialism, if it ever happens. But without overcoming capitalism many of these struggles will have very little chance of succeeding. Only when this simple truth is understood, does democratic unity become possible. It necessarily means creating hierarchy of strategic priorities but at the same time a real equality of people in the movement. This equality must be affirmed through united action, not by separation, through equal opportunities within the common movement, not in a self-made ghetto. We must realize our ecological project, we must affirm women's rights and minorities' rights through and in the process of anti-capitalist struggle, not as a substitution or alternative to it. Finally, this does not mean that other movements, not addressing the central issues of the system, must necessarily be seen as enemies or rivals of socialists. These movements are just as legitimate. Everyone has the same rights. It means simply that no one must expect the socialist left to drop its own culture, tradition and, last but not least, its identity for the sake of 'democratic equivalence'.

To coordinate different struggles a socialist hegemonic project is needed. Chantal Mouffe and Ernesto Laclau use the term 'hegemony' extensively in their writings.[52] What is striking, however, is that it is exactly the hegemonic project which is missing from their writings. No political project is possible without a social agent. Chantal Mouffe and Ernest Laclau never ask themselves a question: where is this agent of hegemony? This is natural because political process for them is completely disconnected from social and economic life. A lot is said about politics but at the same time politics has very little substance. If we go behind the phraseology we discover that hegemony in their discourse means not the capacity of uniting and leading democratically, but rather convergence and compromise.

Of course all this matters only as long as our goal remains to overcome capitalism. If it is not so, all struggles, movements and interests are *really* equal. That is why Chantal Mouffe, like other postmodern radicals, substitutes the socialist perspective with a slogan about broadening democracy (without dropping socialism altogether). There is nothing wrong with that position in principle. The only question is whether capitalism will allow radical democrats to achieve their proclaimed goals. Natural evolution of the system so far has moved us in the opposite direction entirely.

Chantal Mouffe believes in 'liberal socialism'. This means that the socialist tradition must help liberalism to renew itself. She thinks that 'it is necessary to free political liberalism from the hindrances of universalism and individualism. And the socialist tradition can provide insights useful for such a task.'[53] This is not much different from the point of view of Donald Sassoon, who is sure that the only historic task of socialism is to improve capitalism. Naturally Chantal Mouffe speaks about transcending capitalism, while Sassoon presupposes that this is just impossible. But that only means that Sassoon is more consistent.

There is a hidden agent of hegemony, who is never named for the simple reason that the agent is not political. The central figure here is a liberal academic intellectual with a leftist past. And discourse about democratic struggle is just nothing but a Freudian substitute for political action. Lacking political strength of their own, radical democrats expect the socialist struggle to be manipulated towards their goals through supposed 'democratic equivalence'. Thus the democratic rhetoric reveals deeply author- itarian and manipulative intentions, though these are sometimes unconscious.

The labour movement contributed a great deal to broadening democracy, but it was at a time when it was inspired by socialist ideals and anti-capitalist anger, not identity politics. And subor- dinating it now to the project of liberal intellectuals under the banner of 'radical democracy' means stripping it of its own democratic potential, its own culture and tradition.

Universalism and Democracy

The choice of an identity is subjective, and to a significant degree arbitrary. The internal contradictions of a particular person are his or her personal problem, but identity politics makes this a problem of society. The trouble with such an approach is not the fact that it refers to one or another side of someone's individual being, but that a splintering of politics is taking place. Under the influence of identity politics the collective political conscious- ness of radical movements comes to resemble the self-perceptions of a mental patient.

From the point of view of feminism the march of a million black men organized by Louis Farrakhan in Washington in 1995 was a manifestation of 'reactionary sexism'. From the point of racial consciousness it was a giant step forward. Farrakhan's success, however, became possible only because of the crisis of the traditional left movements, which saw the liberation of the black population as being indissolubly linked to the emancipa- tion of the working class. The more each identity group retreats into itself, the more basis it has for complaining that it is mis- understood by others. To criticize one identity or group culture from the position of another makes no sense at all. With the rejection of 'universalism', common criteria disappear. It is not surprising that, in attacking Farrakhan, supporters of feminism resort to thoroughly Marxist arguments, drawing attention to 'the class character of the Million Man March'. Analysis soon reveals the close links between Farrakhan's politics and the interests of minority-owned firms, the African-American business community, and so forth.[54] The trouble is that similar conclusions can be reached if these criteria are applied to most feminist campaigns. Class analysis becomes a sort of bludgeon which can be used against people with opposing views, but which is not to be applied to one's own side. Analysing the social nature of 'friendly' groups is 'class reductionism'. 'Radicalism' and 'conservatism' are transformed into profoundly subjective categories. A totally opportunist principle comes to prevail: the people who are good are those who are with us. And since political relationships change, characterizations change as well.

It is quite natural that there should be contradictions between the women's movement and movements of ethnic groups, between organizations of homosexuals and members of religious and cultural minorities. As such movements develop further, these contradictions will grow more intense. Appeals to solidarity will yield nothing, since unlike the solidarity of the old workers' movement, there is no general interest or common idea at work here. The solidarity that exists can only be of a negative and mechanical type – solidarity in the struggle against a common foe. It does not stand up to serious tests. The establishment is making more and more successful use of such movements against one another and against the left as a whole.

For all its radical-democratic rhetoric, postmodernist ideology has little in common with the democratic movement as this has traditionally been understood. The idea at the heart of democracy has always been equality. If privileges are to be abolished, 'special rights', 'particular status' and so forth are unacceptable. The principle behind citizenship is universalism, even if it is limited in practice by the bounds of the city-state or the country. For a citizen it is natural to orient toward 'the city and the world', since the first is simply a microcosm of the second. But for the postmodernist ideologue the world does not exist, and the city is merely a place where events unfold, a field of action.

Christopher Lasch has remarked aptly that at the very time when the most substantial aspects of democracy are under attack, post-modern radicals are reducing the meaning of democracy to the protection of 'cultural diversity'.[55] Teresa L. Ebert in her brilliant book *Ludic Feminism and After* describes radical feminist theories as 'linguistic play' that cannot present a real challenge to the dominant structures of society. This feminism 'substitutes a politics of representation for radical transformation'.[56]

The polemic waged by the postmodernist left against Enlightenment 'universalism' is fully in line with the logic of liberal tolerance, but scarcely compatible with the ideology of democracy. Ellen Meiksins Wood writes:

> The bourgeoisie challenged the aristocracy by invoking the universal principles of citizenship, civic equality, and the 'nation', a universalistic identity which transcended particular and exclusive identities of kinship, tribe, village, status, estate, or class. In other words, universality was opposed to privilege in its literal meaning as a special or private law – universality as against differential privilege and prescriptive right.

It is not surprising that the universalism of Enlightenment thinking served as a starting-point for the development of socialist ideology: 'For all its limitations, this was an emancipatory universalism.'[57]

Criticism of the ideology of the Enlightenment has become a natural intellectual position flowing out of twentieth-century thought; Enlightenment ideas have shown their limited and authoritarian character. Western concepts of rationality, imposed on societies with different cultures, have been combined with a linear view of social progress and have been used to justify monstrous acts of violence against humanity. But does the criticism of Enlightenment universalism mean that a complete break with it is necessary, or that, on the contrary, we need to work out a new, more profound and diverse concept of 'universalism'?

Defending the traditions of the Enlightenment, Todd Gitlin observes that the Enlightenment 'is self-correcting'. The fact that it remains 'intrinsically incomplete' creates the possibility of new approaches and of an 'open universalism', based on a dialogue of cultures.[58]

This goal cannot be attained without a radical self-criticism by adherents of Enlightenment ideology, something which is just as necessary as self-criticism by socialists. In this sense the attacks by the postmodernists may turn out to be thoroughly beneficial, since they reveal the genuine or imaginary weaknesses of the Enlightenment. But the time for intellectual masochism is vanishing into the past. The task of self-criticism is to affirm the renewal of the Enlightenment and socialist traditions. It is not just the future of the left that depends on this, but also the survival of democracy.

In attacking universalism, supporters of identity politics argue that 'modern racism is one of the "gifts" of the Enlightenment'.[59] The only evidence given for this is a citation of racist texts from the era of the Enlightenment. Texts with an opposing content, even much better known ones, are naturally ignored. The point, however, is not the doubtful validity of this approach, but the fact that, in criticizing the Enlightenment, these writers are consciously or unconsciously shielding capitalism.

Let us begin by noting that xenophobia, slavery and the oppression of members of other tribes or ethnic groups existed long before the era of the Enlightenment. Specifically racist texts were not typical of earlier periods for the simple reason that, until the sixteenth century, Europe had only scant contact with lands inhabited by people of other races. However, it is enough to read Shakespeare's *Othello* to find a whole series of passages testifying to the fact that racist moods also existed in the epoch of the Renaissance.

The history of discrimination against various groups under capitalism shows the degree to which ideology is secondary compared with the system. No one will deny the historic links between slavery and discrimination against blacks in the United States. But the institution of slavery itself was not in any way a product of racism. Slavery appeared on the periphery of the world capitalist system as a result of rapid growth in demand by the centre for cheap agricultural produce and for raw materials for industry. In America in the initial period whites could be slaves just like blacks, and in Russia Orthodox Russian peasants were turned into 'baptized property'. The strengthening of the exploitation of the peasantry in Eastern Europe through serfdom was directly linked to the increasing incorporation of the region into world trade and to the development of capitalism in the West. In America, the possibility of a 'racial' specialization of slavery appeared thanks to the constant influx of slaves from Africa (due in considerable part to the chiefs of coastal tribes in the continent itself). In Eastern Europe and Russia, where there was no such possibility, people were bought and sold without any regard to their culture or race.

The slave trade clearly contradicted the ideology of universalism; because the emerging capitalist system required both one and the other, attempts were made to reconcile the social practice of racial oppression with the general theories of the Enlightenment. These attempts, however, were unsuccessful. All the decisive victories in the struggle against racial discrimination were gained beneath the banner of Enlightenment universalism and of the idea of the equality of citizens that proceeded out of it.

In other words, racism did not give birth to slavery and oppression, but slavery and oppression gave birth to modern racism. It is therefore necessary to struggle not only against racist ideology, but against the system of social institutions and relationships which might in themselves seem quite neutral, but which, in the long run, give rise to racist, anti-semitic and other similar practices.

The Enlightenment concept of citizenship assumed that people were not only equal, but in a certain sense identical. They differed from one another only in their level of knowledge. Strictly speaking, this was simply wrong; people are not identical. But where the state is concerned, the presumption that people are indeed identical has been indispensable; without it, democracy and the equality of citizens before the law would be impossible, and the possibility of vertical mobility would be closed off. While preserving a united hierarchy based on knowledge, the Enlightenment was authoritarian. The need to disseminate knowledge implied not only democracy in the future, but also authoritarian methods in the present, along with the suppression of other cultures or hostility toward them.

In essence, the postmodernists criticize the Enlightenment not from the left but from the right. Despite their refined terminology, their attack on 'universalism' is a sign of the onset of a new barbarism. Whatever neo-liberal theoreticians might say, the reality of the late twentieth century is that the market is destroying civil society. 'Within liberal pluralism, ethnic and racial differences become commodities to be consumed in the marketplace', acknowledges a contributor to *Socialist Review*, which is sympathetic to postmodernism.[60] Identities are themselves being commercialized and institutionalized.

The universalism of the enlighteners was indeed restricted. The trouble is that anti-Enlightenment postmodernist literature attacks not the restricted character of this universalism, but on the contrary, universalism as such! Meanwhile, the authoritarianism and hierarchical nature of the Enlightenment tradition have still to be overcome. Ellen Meiksins Wood correctly stated that:

> to counter the ideological hegemony of the capitalist class . . .
> the task of the theorist is *not* to demonstrate that what *appears*
> universal in bourgeois ideology really *is* universal, having 'no
> precise class connotations' – which is, in effect, precisely to
> accept the hegemonic claims of the dominant class – but rather
> to explain how what appears universal is in fact particular.[61]

This does not mean rejecting universalism as an approach but just going beyond Western bourgeois claims about representing the universal interest and culture.

An orientation to a group or subculture does not by any means signify support for democracy. The narrower the group, and the more it is forced to defend itself from other groups and cultures, the more likely authoritarian and hierarchical tendencies are to develop within it. In order to solve the problems that arise within traditional cultures, it is necessary to find methods that flow out of the historical experience of these cultures themselves. The same is true also of the semi-Western cultures of Eastern Europe and Latin America, where the societies can only dream of being part of the West (this doomed hope is itself an important cultural peculiarity of these societies, one which distinguishes them, say, from China or the Islamic East, where such a problem does not exist). The universalism of the European Enlightenment has played an enormously positive role in the development of 'non-European' peoples, including in their anti-colonial struggles. Precisely because the historico-cultural narrowness of this tradition is obvious, we need to combine and critically reinterpret the new experience accumulated in various countries and cultures thanks to the rise of the new universalism.

Affirmative Action

Rejecting 'universalist' concepts, including Marxism, postmodernist sociology has advanced its own formulae which have been embraced by large numbers of intellectuals disillusioned with socialism. The theory of identity politics has given rise to its own political practice, whose main achievement has been affirmative action, aimed at improving the career prospects of members of oppressed groups within bourgeois society.

Affirmative action transforms the solving of the problems of this or that oppressed group into a task for an enlightened liberal bureaucracy employing 'universal' administrative methods.

American leftists, used to defending the Democrats as a party more sensitive to the interests of minorities, unexpectedly found that 'the greatest gains for affirmative action for Blacks and other oppressed people and women were made under Republican Richard Nixon's presidency in the early 1970s'.[62]

A. Sivanandan, describing the situation in Britain, notes the same tendency. Programmes aimed at helping national and cultural minorities have in practice turned out to be programmes for the formation of a non-white bourgeoisie:

> If opportunity there was, it was opportunity for the 'black' compradors, preened and pruned . . . to blossom into the new 'black' leadership, and later the 'state-class', that would manage racism to keep the lid on protest – or at least deflect it from political struggle.[63]

Programmes of affirmative action that are not linked with 'general' measures for job creation and the democratization of society are at best fraudulent, and at worst are aimed at strengthening the elite.

Social differences play a lesser role here than cultural ones. Significantly, affirmative action has been of very little help to the American black population, whose position has improved scarcely at all during the 1980s and 1990s. In the case of white American women, however, the success of affirmative action has been simply phenomenal. Women have gained important posts in corporations and in state service. Most of these women, however, have been from the upper and middle classes. The social essence of what has happened is obvious. What we see before us is not so much democratization as the restructuring of the system of domination.

As the left feminist Lynne Segal observes:

> The growing immiseration of the US poor was not a product of the failure of feminist equal-rights and affirmative action programmes for women; indeed many succeeded. It resulted

from the now historic weakness of the US labour movement in protecting either male or female workers' rights, or winning any comprehensive welfare system.

In countries where the 'traditional' workers' movement is stronger, the position of women also improved at significantly more rapid rates in the 1980s and 1990s. Consequently, 'it seems perverse to pose women's specific interests *against* rather than *alongside* more traditional socialist goals'.[64]

This argument, however, makes sense only if we accept the claims of radical feminism to speak for all women. If, on the other hand, we examine things from the point of view of the middle class, the picture becomes somewhat different. An alliance with organized labour was valuable for dispossessed groups within the middle class so long as the workers' movement was on the rise. As soon as it became clear that a bloc with socialist forces would not bring a quick outcome, a process of reorientation began. This was expressed in an ideological shift to the right – in the defending of 'specific' interests, in identity politics and in radical feminism. Attempts by leftists to keep the rightward-drifting 'new social movements' within their orbit through ever-new ideological concessions and symbolic gestures brought nothing except a still greater erosion of the traditional socialist bloc. The only thing leftists could do in such a situation, if they wanted such allies back at all, was to become stronger themselves.

The Eastern European experience, for all its specific features, carries the same message. The system of quotas and of 'representation' was developed extensively in the Soviet Union and other countries of the communist bloc. The starting point was the same as in the West – a desire to correct the injustice and inequality that had existed in bourgeois-landlord Russia. Quotas ensured the 'priority' of members of various nationalities (who had earlier been discriminated against) for promotion to particular posts. The same methods were also used in the struggle for women's rights. It would be wrong to argue that these methods did not at first have positive results. By no means the least important reason for the rapid growth of the Soviet economy in the 1930s and 1950s was an astonishing degree of social mobility. The new prospects that opened up before millions of people who had earlier been doomed to a secondary role in society stimulated labour enthusiasm, innovativeness and selflessness. By the end of the Soviet era women made up 40 per cent of scientists and technicians and 40 per cent of leaders in elective positions, compared with 8 per cent in the US. However, Soviet women were denied entry to the top party elite, and the women who were accepted into the *nomenklatura* remained a sort of secondary category, something that was reflected in the composition and psychology of this layer. By the end of the 1960s, quotas had become an organic part of the conservative Soviet *nomenklatura* system. Groups had become established that controlled and defended their quotas. In addition, new injustices had begun to accumulate, affecting groups which had not been included in the quota structures earlier.

The number of women in the lower and middle levels of the bureaucracy was very high, but there was little joy for Soviet women in this situation. This is why the reactionary wave of the 1990s, when high-ranking officials proclaimed that women should stay at home and raise children, did not arouse serious resistance. Bureaucratic methods of solving the 'woman question' meant that when 'progress' engineered from above was replaced by reaction from the same source, there was no one to struggle against it.

The implanting of conservative values in society, along with the growth of poverty and unemployment among women, did not by any means signify the disappearance of the female *nomen-klatura*. Quite the reverse. The worse the position of the majority of women became, the more important and influential the bureaucracy that sought to speak on their behalf. The successor in Yeltsin's Russia to the Soviet practice of 'advancement' was the activity of the organization Women of Russia. In its rhetoric, this body managed a paradoxical mix of feminist, patriarchal and bureaucratic values. Women of Russia leader Yekaterina Lakhova expressed this in exquisite fashion when she declared: 'On the professional level, the interests of women, of the family and of children can be defended only by women.'[65]

In the 1993 elections the Women of Russia list, consisting of high-placed women bureaucrats, won election to the State Duma, where its deputies revealed a total indifference to the problems of women. In most cases, the Western feminist press greeted the victory of Women of Russia with unconcealed enthusiasm. And indeed, this organization had achieved what many Western feminists had sought unsuccessfully: the Russian parliament had a women's fraction. It is true that Women of Russia had succeeded precisely because its members were not feminists. Their ideology, if one can speak of ideas in relation to such a group, was profoundly traditionalist, oriented toward such values as respect for the state, a strong governing authority, a stable family and a powerful army.

Unlike Western commentators, Russian leftists from the very first saw in Women of Russia a hostile and dangerous organization. After some vacillation, many Russian feminists also began to show hostility to Women of Russia. 'A new female *nomenklatura*', Nadezhda Azhgikhina wrote in *Nezavisimaya Gazeta*, 'is arising before our eyes.' The women's congresses and other initiatives undertaken by the movement, Azhgikhina argued, were aimed at achieving a single goal: to have women 'formally, even if in a whisper, express support for the authorities'. Meanwhile, the authorities let it be known that they were sympathetic, and were lending an ear to the hopes of 'these little ones'. The formation of a female clientele around the apparatus of power became an important element in the policies of the ruling elite, at a time when life was becoming more and more difficult for most women. However, this proved insufficient for Women of Russia to consolidate its success. In the 1995 elections the organization failed to reach the cut-off point needed for its candidates to be elected. As Azhgikhina noted, 'women would not vote for a movement that lacked social support apart from the women's councils'.[66]

Is this situation unique to Russia? By no means. Pat Brewer notes a direct link between Western theories of 'power feminism' and the struggle for jobs and influence within the establishment. The theories can be very pretentious.

> More prosaic is the spectacle of liberal feminists who, as they pursue their careers in government bureaucracy, academia, parliament and the managerial echelons of private corporations, draw on difference theories to justify their 'trail blazing' into male institutions: what 'sister' could deny them understanding and support as they rush to have their turn at the relevant trough?[67]

Liberal women, occupying top-level posts in the establishment, are themselves becoming an obstacle in the struggle for the rights of women.

> All forms of bourgeois feminism have been strengthened over the last decade. Those who fought for the reforms that have been won up to date – many of whom are former socialist feminists who now turned social-democratic neo-liberals in the unions and the Labor parties – are increasingly pessimistic, silenced and inactive. Unable to speak out and to mobilise because this would jeopardise their careers, they look instead to the appointment of high profile women to positions of parliamentary or bureaucratic 'power' as the realistic way to stop the backlash against feminism.[68]

From Defensive Struggles to Corporatism

By the mid-1990s 'radical democracy', identity politics and affirmative action had become transformed from offensive strategies into defensive ones. The neo-liberal political strategy included the encouragement of 'diversity' within the framework of the 'open society', but only so long as 'diversity' and cultural pluralism were necessary as a means of struggle against 'standardizing' and 'depersonalizing' communism. In the conditions of the mid-1990s the attitude of the elites to the various programmes aimed at defending the interests of minorities changed. On the one hand, communism had been defeated on the world scale. But on the other, economic liberalization and privatization meant that the quantity of resources that could be diverted for social and cultural programmes had diminished sharply. In this situation, affirmative action had been transformed from a means of correcting the injustices of society into an attempt to hold back the neo-conservative wave and to retain for specific groups the positions they had won.

The practice of affirmative action is closely linked to the absence or enfeeblement of the institutions of civil democracy. The practice of modern bourgeois society is increasingly leading us away from the Enlightenment ideology of civic equality toward medieval concepts of specific rights, liberties and privileges possessed by each particular social group. These groups are fundamentally unequal. The difference in rights makes a single democratic process impossible, and inevitably assumes the presence of a supreme arbiter who maintains the harmony and balance between numerous specific groups and corporations. In addition, every community and category of no-longer-citizens needs its own corporate formation representing its interests before this arbiter, and recognized by the arbiter as a partner. There is no doubting that the differences between people and groups are absolutely real; this is why the principle of divide and rule is effective.

'Multiculturalism deflected the political concerns of the black community into the cultural concerns of different communities, the struggle against racism into the struggle for culture', writes A. Sivanandan in a book on the struggle against racism in Britain. 'Government funding of self-help groups undermined the self-reliance, the self-created social and economic base, of those groups: they were no longer responsive to or responsible for the people they served – and service itself became a profitable concern.'[69]

Corporative authoritarianism is the logical outcome of such pluralism. Ensuring a certain freedom for the expression of group egoism, society leaves no openings for democracy. From bourgeois individualism we make the shift to something far more archaic and dangerous.

Defending the policy of affirmative action, Stephen Steinberg writes in *New Politics*: 'The significance of affirmative action is that it constitutes a frontal attack on institutionalized racism.'[70] Here we find expressed the very essence of the approach: affirmative action does not lead to the eradication of racism, but proposes to eliminate its consequences, as one institution against another. This provides a perfect analogy for the social democratic attitude to the free market and private property: eliminating the imbalances within the system while retaining the system. Unlike the social democrats, of course, radical currents from time to time recall their hostility toward the capitalist system. As one of the participants in a public discussion in New York in the autumn of 1995 put it, 'Affirmative action doesn't solve everything, let's have a revolution.'[71] But in between affirmative action and 'revolution', there is a vacuum. The first is concerned with the 'bad present', and the second with the 'shining future'. To move directly from one to the other is impossible in principle, but intermediate stages are not suggested. Sometime or other, revolution will simply solve all the problems at a blow. In the meantime, people must live by the laws of the capitalist world, trying as best they can to 'compensate' for its injustices, trailing submissively in the wake of the liberal establishment and not experiencing any pangs of conscience.

Left-wing adherents of identity politics stress that their programme should be understood not as a refusal to raise social demands, but 'as conceiving cultural recognition as a means to economic and political justice', at the same time as they call for 'recognition for the sake of redistribution'.[72] The problem, however, is that struggling for redistribution within the bounds of the system is itself a dead-end. The history of social democracy has already shown this quite well. Only where redistribution has been the consequence of structural reforms, including reforms that affect property relations, has it had any major social consequences. Identity politics and affirmative action fail precisely because the logic of social relationships cannot be annulled through liberal resolutions. Injustices and imbalances are reproduced again and again. At best, the structure of the capitalist elite will change somewhat, but the winner from this will be the elite itself, benefiting from a modest infusion of 'new blood'.

Leftist Strategies

In the short term, affirmative action can represent a correct tactical choice, like many other measures applied by social democracy or the Soviet system. As a first step toward improving the situation, it is simply indispensable. Criticizing the 'Great Russian chauvinism' of Stalin and other Moscow comrades in 1922, Lenin demanded positive discrimination in favour of national and religious minorities. This was absolutely correct. In South Africa, after black Africans had not been employed for many years in the state public service, it was not enough simply to proclaim formal equality; a special policy had to be implemented in the interests of blacks. To cease applying affirmative action is in principle as illogical as to regard it as a panacea. To the growing criticism of affirmative action from the right, socialists need to counterpose not useless attempts to defend liberal policies, but their own radical criticism, demanding structural reforms. Leftists have to recognize affirmative action as a half-measure, inadequate and contradictory, that does not solve the problems of the oppressed sectors of the population. It is essential to think through the possibilities and limitations of such methods. However, the supporters of affirmative action often react in aggressive and insulted fashion not only to criticism of their approach, but even to discussion of it. For these people, affirmative action was long ago transformed from a tactic into an ideology, providing moral justification for their rejection of efforts to bring about serious social change ('Look, we're doing what we can'). Any doubts as to the effectiveness of such an approach evoke an extremely pained, neurotic response.

For right-wing social democrats the ideas of identity politics, feminism, 'civil society' and 'radical democratization' are becoming political life-savers, allowing these people to claim that their movement is still trying to change society. Privileges for the elites that head the minorities are needed in order to guarantee corporate-clientelist support from these constituencies. The Australian Labor Party (ALP), traditionally among the most right-wing of labour organizations, has made the 'culture of difference' its key slogan in the 1990s. As the Australian *Green Left Weekly* notes:

> The 'culture of difference' was the essence of the ALP's multicultural agenda: to value the 'other' without challenging the social relations which relegate those others to the bottom of the social heap, from where they rarely rise. While it gave tacit support to the aspirations of ethnic groups through grants programs, the ALP cut immigration intakes and frog-marched 'illegal' refugees off to remote camps.[73]

In essence such policies are not markedly different from the open corporatism of Women of Russia, although the rhetoric and style are quite different.

Just as the crisis of the traditional left has been closely connected with the erosion of the welfare state, the rise of the new corporatism and of identity politics has been inseparable from the aggressive implementation of the ideology of 'civil society'. Until the 1980s the concept of 'civil society' was best known as one of the themes of Western Marxism, which rests on the later works of Gramsci. Marx and Gramsci borrowed the term from Hegel, who could never have been described as a radical. Since the 1980s the idea of civil society has come to be widely used in the writings of liberal ideologues. Postmodernist socialism and neo-liberalism are as one in their denial of the key role of the state in the process of social change. While using the term 'civil society', postmodernist radicalism understands it in a way quite different from Gramsci. For the Italian Marxist, the state and civil society were closely interconnected, and the idea of replacing the one with the other would have seemed an obvious absurdity. Gramsci conceived of democracy as a type of state resting on a developed civil society, unlike 'Eastern' governments which in the absence of civil society, themselves carried out its functions. The new radicalism sees this question entirely the other way round.

In parallel with the growing interest in specific groups, we have seen the development of a sort of cult of republican values, emptied, however, of their original 'universalist' content and often combined with the idea of the 'limitation of the role of the state'. In Britain and Australia the loss of socialist perspectives among leftists has been accompanied by the growth of a quasi-republican radicalism. Thus Will Hutton, one of the leaders of the movement Charter 88, considers that even if the monarchy is retained, 'Britain needs what might be called a republican attitude to its culture and institutions.'[74]

The coming to power of post-communist social democracy in Poland in 1993 was linked not only with the nostalgia for the past that has appeared everywhere in Eastern Europe, but also with the fact that the social democrats were seen as guaranteeing the survival of the secular state, equal rights for women and other conquests of the 'modern age' that were under fire from clerical obscurantism. But as the French political scientist Bruno Drweski notes, the 'modernism' of the post-communist left in Poland 'does not exclude a certain timidity toward the Catholic church'.[75]

The left is thus acting not as a force campaigning for social reform, but as the final bastion (and at times not an especially solid one) of modernism, republicanism and rationalism. How this can be combined with criticism of the Enlightenment and of universalism is a problem of theoretical consciousness that does not upset practical activists unduly. Rejecting the struggle against bourgeois society, leftists are inclined to take on the 'unfinished

work' of the bourgeois revolution, which the ruling class itself
has refused to force through to completion. In other words, the
task of 'radicals' is reduced to making bourgeois society even
more bourgeois. Here, however, there are insurmountable
obstacles. Classical republicanism is no longer especially
attractive to the bourgeoisie itself, while the lower strata of
society, suffering from the effects of social crisis, remain
indifferent to this struggle, since they do not see any direct link
between it and their own current problems. Under pressure from
the advancing barbarism, therefore, the modernist left surrenders
one position after another.

For some time the question of the social nature of the state has
ceased to arouse interest, just like the question of the character
and structure of 'civil society' itself. Everything is reduced to such
essentially 'neutral' and 'technical' concepts as 'complexity',
'multi-level structure' and so forth, though in fact any idea of the
essence and social tasks of the various political mechanisms
disappears behind these secondary characteristics. 'Never before
has it been so necessary to regulate complexity by means of
decisions, choices and "policies", the frequency and diffusion of
which must be ensured if the uncertainty of systems subject to
exceptionally rapid change is to be reduced.'[76] In sum, the very
concept of change has to be altered. 'Change in complex societies
becomes discontinuous, articulated, differentiated.' Changes are
ceasing to amount to transformations. 'Changes within a
complex system are always changes of adaptive type; while they
may also entail ruptures, these changes always pertain to the
overall systemic balance.'[77] Traditional parties and state institutions cannot cope with this; the time has come for 'civil society'.

While some speak of the growing complexity and heterogeneity of society, others argue with no less conviction that 'the
uniformity of thought' is taking on unprecedented scope, and
that global standardization is affecting even 'cultural diasporas'.[78]
Such ideological monoliths cannot arise on the basis of a genuine
diversity; they appear only if the whole variety of interests has at
its base a common foundation in the form of a particular system
of power relationships. The changes occurring on the surface
scarcely affect it. But with every cycle of development everything
becomes more complex and obscure; not only is formal
democracy deprived of any meaning, but the functioning of civil
society and of social movements loses its point as well. The more

complex the system, the less comprehensible is its logic, and the greater the scope for manipulation; the less access citizens have to information, the less they understand their place in society. A labyrinth cannot be transparent, by definition.

The task of democratic change is precisely to bring about a radical simplification of the system. When capitalism disappears along with its system of rule, many specific interests will disappear at the same time. The identities which we are now being urged to maintain and strengthen will disappear or be transformed as well.

Non-government Organizations

The politics of specific interests, identities and single issues no longer require traditional-type organizations, whether parties, trade unions or even mass movements. The 'new social movements' are notable for being neither 'social' (in the sense of representing some relatively broad social layer), nor movements. The place of mass organizations is taken by specialized groups and by a network of 'non-government organizations' (NGOs). The question is not whether the goals of these organizations are good or bad. The mass environmental movement of the mid-1970s has been replaced by the expensive professional actions of Greenpeace, and the anti-war movement has switched from organizing mass marches to holding symposiums and to lobbying high-placed officials. This activity may be socially useful, or it may amount to no more than extracting funds for the support of the movement's own apparatus. In any case, it is the apparatus which serves as the central element of the new politics.

The professionalization of the NGOs also presents enticing prospects for radical activists who have grown tired of poverty and self-sacrifice. The leader of the radical Russian organization Student Defence, Dmitriy Petrov, published a veritable panegyric to NGOs on the pages of *Nezavisimaya Gazeta*:

> Their resources are great, their policies are transnational, and their strategies are long-term. Privileges in areas such as taxation and customs help them attract impressive sums in contributions. The people who contribute include both American and European wage-earners and large corporations.

Show business super-stars organize festivals to aid children in Africa. . . .

Non-governmental organizations are seen as combining humanism and 'new advertising opportunities'; they are:

> becoming the last hope of angry students, of embittered workers driven to despair by their impoverishment, of lonely old people, of the sick and homeless, of abandoned children, of minorities deprived of their rights. They are spurring a revival of civilized values, of the progressive traditions of community-mindedness, of collective leadership and mutual support. They are giving strength to the powerless.[79]

In reality, such organizations could not exist if they did not have close links with the state, which effectively transfers to them part of its own functions and at the same time removes from itself responsibility for the results of its activity.[80] On the one hand, lobbying, corporatism and paternalism are becoming the basis for the new social movements. On the other, there is a partial privatization of civil life and even of the social sphere. This is far more dangerous for democracy and citizenship than traditional corporatism. Corruption represents a natural continuation of such policies. It was no accident that the comprehensively corrupt regime of 'socialist' Bettino Craxi in Italy had close links with NGOs, receiving political support from them in exchange for financial aid and at the same time promoting them as an alternative to the 'old left'.

The 'new social movements' and NGOs began with a justified criticism of the centralism, authoritarianism and bureaucratism of the 'old' labour movement, of its parties, trade unions and mass organizations. They finished up being transformed into narrow groups of professionals, completely outside the control of the majority of the population and dependent on external sources of funding. Bureaucracy is an inevitable evil in any organization. The only thing that makes it possible to limit this evil is a system of democratic control, something which existed, even if only to a limited degree, in the traditional mass parties. It was precisely for this reason that the bourgeoisie needed a considerable time to integrate the labour movement elite into the establishment. The organizations themselves have never been integrated fully; from time to time even the most 'tame' and 'moderate' trade unions and workers' parties present the ruling hierarchs with unpleasant surprises. By contrast, the new social movements and NGOs were integrated quickly, easily and almost completely. Their striking success in the mid-1990s was a symptom of their powerlessness.[81]

The evolution of the environmental movement in Russia provides an excellent example. During the *perestroika* years environmental actions were a very important part of the new civil and social initiatives. Theorists of the movement declared proudly that these actions were turning 'the population' into citizens. In protesting against the pollution of the environment, it was said, people voluntarily assumed 'responsibility for carrying out activity, considering this to be their duty as citizens'.[82]

After three years members of the Social-Ecological Union of Russia noted a decline in the movement. Although the state of the environment had deteriorated noticeably, people who were worn down by the difficulties of surviving in the conditions of 'savage capitalism' were no longer ready either to take part in protests or to join environmental organizations. Ideologues of the movement recognized that a 'serious crisis' had arisen. Leading environmentalists were observed to be vacillating between positions as allies and opponents of the system, and the basis of solidarity actions had been undermined. The realities of the mid-1990s were:

> bureaucratization, social differentiation and hierarchization, a growing gap between the core of the movement and its periphery, the concentrating of the functions of resource distribution in the hands of leaders, and independence of their actions with relation to rank and file activists.[83]

In the space of fifteen years, the new social movements, not only in Russia but also in the West, followed the same trajectory of bureaucratization and decline that the old workers' movement had taken one and a half centuries to trace out. The lack of a clear class base helped ensure the accelerated decay of the 'radical' political elites. In Russia, the leaders of the environmental movement managed to avoid many of the temptations connected with participation in power and with corruption. The accelerated decay of Russian environmentalism was linked not only to its own internal problems, but also to the general failure of civil society, which perished even before it had managed to appear. Environmentalism was an expression of civil activism, and went into decline along with it. For lack of a powerful social impulse this civic activism could neither be reborn from below, nor be implanted from above.

Unable to mobilize a massive social base, the environmental organizations put their faith in the work of professionals. In the conditions of Russia this meant orienting toward Western financial help: 'The movement's structure changed because its financing priorities were still determined by Western experts and organizations.' Radical ideas and moods gave way to pragmatism.

> Grant-giving organizations finance only 'constructive' projects, thereby strengthening the reformist character of the movement. The disintegration in the movement is enhanced under such conditions. If a certain project wins financial support for a certain length of time, then the group receiving the grant is locked into its implementation. In this scenario intergroup solidarity abates and intergroup competition surges.[84]

The fundamental logic of ecological politics must lead to a confrontation with capitalist monopolies, profit-oriented production and the market system. However, particular environmentalist organizations need financing, Green parties look for influential partners and Green politicians for ministerial positions. In other words they get more and more subordinated to the logic of the system against which they have to fight. They swallow the myth of environmentally safe capitalism and tell us that big business is going to be 'at the cutting edge of the move to a clean, green economy'.[85] That leads environmentalist groups to all sorts of unrealistic and even demagogic proposals as in the cartoon *Captain Planet* where the viewers, in order to help save the Earth, are seriously advised not to turn on their air conditioning when it gets hot.

Class Politics comes Back

In the late 1980s any criticism of postmodernist radicalism and feminism was taboo among Western leftists. Ellen Meiksins

Wood, who in her works systematically criticized postmodernist radicalism, found herself virtually isolated. Even among supporters of traditional Marxism, efforts to avoid such discussions were the rule. By the mid-1990s the situation had changed. This was the result both of the increasingly obvious turn to the right by the ideologues of identity politics and feminism, and of the failure of the policies that had been pursued under their influence (including, in matters concerning the rights of women and minorities, under their direct influence). Under fire from critics, the supporters of identity politics were forced onto the defensive, while authoritative left-wing writers spoke their minds quite openly and bluntly.

Eric Hobsbawm wrote in *New Left Review*:

> Human beings cannot be described, even for bureaucratic purposes, except by a combination of many characteristics. But identity politics assumes that one among many identities we all have is the one that determines, or at least dominates our politics: being a woman, if you are a feminist, being a Protestant if you are an Antrim Unionist, being a Catalan, if you are a Catalan nationalist, being homosexual if you are in the gay movement. And, of course, that you have to get rid of the others, because they are incompatible with the 'real' you.

People in this way are forced to make an absurd choice, which they cannot make without damaging the fullness and complexity of their personalities. 'It is more likely to be forced upon them from outside – in the way in which Serb, Croat and Muslim inhabitants of Bosnia who lived together, socialized together and intermarried, have been forced to separate, or in less brutal ways.'[86]

In his book *The Twilight of Common Dreams*, the American Todd Gitlin notes that the success of Reagan and the Republican right in the 1980s was conditioned to a significant degree by their ability to provide society with a unifying mythology, capable of mobilizing a massive social base of conservatives. The Democrats and the left, by constrast, were unable to put forward anything that might have unified their heterogeneous social base.

> The Democrats were a loose, baggy party, the Left an aggregation of movements, grouplets, and ideological

tendencies, both suffering from a disproportion of margins to center. Both now amounted to collections of interest groups and little more, and lacked a vocabulary for the common good. Both had shed the custom of affirming the whole people. Not only were they ethnically and racially diverse, and so especially vulnerable to centrifugal tendencies, but in the New Deal tradition, they had believed in government spending as a social binder, an instrument of justice, a means to reduce inequality and a defence of the middle class all at once. Without the Cold War, growing numbers of Americans now asked, what was the positive point of the government? It was seen as an instrument of division, a plaything of 'special interests', a broken machinery – or an ogre.[87]

The problem, of course, did not lie in any inability of the state to serve as a shield for 'special interests', correcting various injustices and social imbalances. But the state could only do this effectively if it embodied a universalist, unifying idea, in the name of which all redistributive efforts were undertaken. Such an idea was present in the New Deal and the welfare state, but it is not and cannot be present in identity politics.

The right wing that has consolidated itself on the basis of neo-liberalism is confronted by a fragmented and ideologically amorphous left movement. Of the ideology of the left there remains only a 'shapeless melange' which is linked to Marxism only 'sentimentally'.[88] The rejection of universalism and of the class approach has led to the fragmentation of the left movement itself. The left has lost not only its common reference points and clear general goals, but also its link to the democratic tradition and to the ideas of citizenship and equality. It was universalist values that inspired the first fighters for civil rights, whether these were the rights of women or of national minorities. With the rejection of this, all demands and struggles were 'privatized' by particular groups – in precise accordance with the logic of neo-liberalism. Civic action was reduced at best to 'lobbying from below'.

Every separate movement maintained that, in the final analysis, it served the common good. But the idea of the common good was not central for it, and such statements were therefore perceived as 'rhetorical fillips, pious afterthoughts'.[89] Only environmentalists were willing to pose the question of general rather than specific interests in an important way, and it was this which to a significant degree was responsible for their success. But disowning such concepts as class, labour and capital as irrelevant to their cause, they refused to join in the founding of a united front to include the trade unions and traditional workers' parties. They proved unable to work out their own concept of structural reforms, even though the destruction of nature was due not to 'environmental illiteracy', but to the logic of the system.[90]

Gitlin's book summoned up a storm of indignation on the American left. But the strongest argument against it was that Gitlin and other writers who criticized identity politics were 'angry white men',[91] who should therefore not be trusted. Some of the most aggressive of the book's critics were themselves white men, but white men who were 'ashamed' of their biological status.

It is instructive to note that at their first encounter with criticism, the people who were condemning Marxism, the Enlightenment and the labour movement as intolerant of 'difference' resorted to totally Stalinist polemical methods. Other writers, by contrast, reiterated that they did not in principle deny the existence of classes or even 'the struggle to dismantle capitalism', but recalled that class was simply another identity like all the others, and that consequently it could not be elevated 'above these other identities'. [92] The point, however, is that class identity unlike all other identities was created by the capitalist system and by it alone. All identity is social, but class is the quintessence of the social. Unlike race, sex, culture or place of birth, class cannot be determined except by the position of the individual in society, and cannot be reproduced except through participation in the functioning of the economic system. Class politics is possible only within the framework of capitalism; it was created by capitalism and is reproduced together with it, and for this reason poses a real danger to it.

The most serious argument in defence of identity politics boils down to maintaining that one should speak out against identity politics from the left so long as it is under attack from the right, and that criticizing postmodernist radicalism 'does not promote solidarity'.[93] From the theoretical point of view this argument is absurd; the truth does not depend on the political conjuncture. But the call to solidarity is not completely convincing either. If the majority of leftists can be reproached for anything, it is for their refusal, for the sake of solidarity, to criticize identity politics throughout most of the 1980s and the first half of the 1990s. Growing criticism from the left and right has been an inevitable result of the failures of identity politics. These failures are all the more striking for the fact that the ideology of identity politics remained unchallenged for at least a decade, while its supporters enjoyed unprecedented openings for propaganda.

Against the background of the weakening of the traditional workers' movement, the overall relationship of forces has changed. By aiding the demoralization of the workers' movement, the supporters of postmodernist radicalism have strengthened the bourgeoisie, which now rewards them with ingratitude. The supporters of identity politics make an assiduous pretence of not knowing a simple, obvious fact: that the quantity of resources and activists at the disposal of the left is extremely limited. This means that in conditions when neo-liberalism threatens the very bases of people's normal human existence, these resources and strengths should not be dispersed over a range of 'different, but equal struggles', but should be concentrated as far as possible on the main lines of resistance. Neo-liberal politicians know this, and do not squander their energies on trifles. They turned their fire against the supporters of identity politics only after dealing with the labour movement, and they concern themselves with identity politics only to the extent to which it hinders them in carrying out specific tasks.

The theoreticians of the culture of difference are not to blame for the burdensome position in which the left movement now finds itself. The real guilt lies with the communist and social-democratic bureaucracies, with the capitulating intellectuals, and with the workers' movement itself and its tradition of 'factory discipline'. But the way out of the present crisis should not be sought where identity politics, postmodernist radicalism and belated republicanism indicate. In this sense, these phenomena are obstacles on the road to the future.

As Colin Leys and Leo Panitch write in *Socialist Register*:

> What has always been missing – and now strongly felt by many social movement leaders themselves – is something that would be more than the sum of the parts, something which the Social Democratic and Communist parties did partly

provide in their heyday . . . . These include providing activists with a strategic, ideological and educational vehicle; a political home which is open to individuals to enter (rather than restricted, as today's social movement networking is, to representatives of groups); a political community which explicitly seeks to transcend the particularistic identities while supporting and building on the struggles they generate.[94]

The alternative to the politics of bureaucratic philanthropy has to be sought in the struggle for decentralization, in work in communities, in the strengthening of local self-government, in the struggle to create jobs, in public investment and in education. Equal rights will become a reality only as a result of all-round reforms that change the logic of social reproduction. Structural reforms do not solve cultural problems, but they create the conditions in which solving these problems becomes a serious possibility. The struggle for a culture of difference solves neither economic nor cultural problems. It merely forces us into a vicious circle of attempts to treat the symptoms of society's illness.

The left began with the slogan of changing society from below. Reforms are impossible except through the state, but this in no way signifies that their essence has to consist of bureaucratic decision-making. On the contrary, it is essential to create conditions under which people have less need of being 'defended' by the state and are better able to look after themselves. The point is simply that the road to this does not lie through the 'free market', nor through the philanthropy of NGOs and the lobbying of interest groups, but through social changes that free people from the power of capital and from control by the 'invisible hand' of the ruling class.

3

The Third Left or the Third Socialism

In the mid-1990s, during a debate on the programme of the Finnish Left Union, the economist Jan Otto Andersson formulated the idea of the 'third left'. According to Andersson, the 'first left' was the bourgeois republican movement, which demanded liberty from absolutist and feudal fetters, called for equality through the abolition of rank and privilege, and extolled brotherhood over the power of the masters. It was 'the Left of liberty, citizenship, democracy'.[1] The 'second left' was the working-class socialism of social-democratic and communist parties. This left struggled for economic and social rights and was the main vehicle of the welfare state project. It favoured collective solutions to social problems, and saw nationalization and planning as means toward a more just and progressive society.

The 'Third Left'

The 'third left', in Andersson's view, now has to combine the values of radical democracy, human rights and socialism.

> The Third Left necessarily builds on the traditions of the First and Second, as it transcends them. Its earliest manifestation was the New Left of the 1960s, followed by the environmental and feminist movements of the 1970s. This Left was able to think more globally, to listen more attentively to the demands of oppressed peoples, and to respect divergence more readily than the old Left. It was not, however, able to take advantage of the crisis of Fordist capitalism. Instead, it had to watch the triumph of neo-liberalism and neo-conservatism.[2]

According to Andersson, it will become a coherent political force only when it has grasped the full implications of the dramatic transformations of the past two decades: the shaking of the advanced industrial societies, the hollowing out of the national welfare states and the collapse of Soviet communism.

The Spanish sociologist Jaime Pastor also speaks of the birth of a 'third left', which will be 'anticapitalist and oriented toward change'. Making a critical assessment of the Soviet and Chinese experience, Pastor concludes that:

> this left has to be ready to renew both the content and the forms of political action, beginning with the political party form itself and continuing with the subordination of institutional action to the recreating of an alternative social fabric and to changes in behaviour in the 'world of daily life'.

As Pastor admits, 'we are still a long way from this'.[3]

It is not hard to see that despite using similar terminology, the various writers have different things in mind. Andersson stresses the need for leftists to arm themselves with the liberating ideas of early bourgeois democracy, while Pastor urges an anticapitalist alternative formulated in a new way.

The world left is indeed moving into a new stage. But what is the real political content of the term 'third left'? The historical project of bourgeois-democratic radicalism was on the whole realized successfully, at least in Western Europe, but working-class socialism has met with failure. This has been true not only of Soviet communism, but also of the social democratic vision of the welfare state. It is impossible to see a strategic perspective for the left simply in a mechanistic combining of the values of radical democracy with socialist principles, especially since such a combination has already been typical of the socialist movement for many years.

Furthermore, the failure of the 'second left' has placed in doubt the values of the 'first left' as well. In a world in which democratic principles receive almost universal lip service, the 1990s have seen an obvious weakening of democratic institutions in the traditionally 'free' countries. Historically, the workers' movement has not been in the least bit hostile to democracy. It was born out of the democratic movement, and played a decisive role in the conquest and defence of civil liberties.[4] In many countries it was the labour movement that forced the introduction of universal suffrage and republican constitutions, while compelling the abolition of various limitations on political activity. Tragically, leftists in the final years of the century are at times being forced to discover the values of democracy afresh, but this is not yet a guarantee of renewal.

The 'Third Socialism'

While Jan Otto Andersson was talking of a 'third left', Samir Amin was putting into circulation the term 'a third socialism'. In Amin's view, the first socialism belongs to the nineteenth century. This was the socialism of the epoch of the steam engine and of early industrialization, the socialism of the first and second internationals. Its time came to an end in 1914. The second socialism was born of the world wars and of Fordist technologies of mass production. It died along with the Soviet system. The time of the third socialism is now beginning. This is the socialism of the epoch of globalization and computer technology. In these new conditions the socialist movement cannot be other than internationalist, and at the same time it must aim 'to rebuild a polycentric world, thus providing scope for the people's autonomous progress'. Samir Amin has stressed that such a transition cannot occur spontaneously; it requires the action of a political force: 'One I described as revolutionary, although possible through a range of consistent reforms; it entailed a certain ideological consciousness capable of expressing the demands of a new social project.'[5] Unless this transition is carried through, humanity will come up against the growing crisis and degeneration of the global capitalist system, which is unable either to cope with the contradictions to which it has given birth, or to reform itself. The sole alternative to socialism remains barbarism – 'decadence of society, through redoubled violence of senseless conflicts'. In this sense Rosa Luxemburg's formula 'socialism or barbarism' is more timely than ever.[6]

Neither Andersson nor Amin identifies the new socialism with the labour movement. In their view, the new socialist project should encompass a broad spectrum of social forces on a global level. In a certain sense their approaches complement one another.[7] At the same time, the social and political configuration of the new bloc remains quite diffuse, and the strategy and programme for its concrete actions unclear.

It would be unfair to demand of theoreticians a precise programme for a movement which is still only in its germinal stages. The trouble is that the efforts of radical ideologues to formulate goals on the most general level leave room not only for different interpretations, but also for directly opposite ones. The idea of the 'third left' can lie at the basis of a broad anti-capitalist bloc oriented toward reform, or it may be used as a self-justification by politicians with a radical past who are seeking a comfortable existence within the parliamentary system. In exactly the same way, the idea of the 'third socialism' may become a reference-point for practical action, or may remain simply the theme of academic discussions. In neither instance is there a clear answer to the most painful and perhaps most important question: what needs to be discarded from the heritage of the traditional left, and what should be retained? In what form will the historical values and goals of socialism be realized in a changed world?

The new phase in the development of the left movement is beginning in slow and tormented fashion. The crisis of neo-liberalism has not sparked revolutionary outbursts. There are instances in which left parties again enjoy mass support and even hold the political initiative, but these parties now often lack not only revolutionary strategies, but even reformist ones.

The fact that leftists are coming to power signifies that the elites are in crisis. But are the forces of the left ready to present an alternative? Here we are once again forced to return to the problem of radical reformism. Where does the border lie between radical reformism and elementary opportunism on the one side, and between radical reforms and revolution on the other? An obvious and rigid dividing line simply does not exist, but there are fundamental differences. These need to be clearly formulated, especially now, when in many countries revolutionary organizations are proclaiming the slogan of a 'turn to reformism' while in fact rejecting serious reforms.

The reason for the failure of the majority of reformist projects during recent years has been their 'top-down' character. In this sense Mitterrand as the bearer of the ideas of the technocratic elite and Gorbachev, resting on the 'enlightened' section of the Soviet bureaucracy, were equally remote from the people they promised to make happy.

Among the reactions to the failures of reformist and revolutionary parties were calls for replacing them with 'new mass movements', and for substituting 'alternatives from below' for 'policies from above'. At the Budapest conference of left theoreticians in 1994, speakers even raised the concept of 'de-linking from below'[8] as an economic alternative to neo-liberal globalization.

It can easily be seen that all this is no more than a mirror image of previous illusions. The state is hierarchical, and the world system is vertically integrated. These structures were specially created in order to resist pressures from below. Any effective mass movement gives birth to its own hierarchical structure – in the final analysis, to its own 'counter-elite'. It is not hard to see that under certain conditions this 'counter-elite' can become integrated into the 'establishment', but this does not by any means signify that it is possible to do without it entirely.

The radical-reformist answer to these appeals can only be to try to unite the 'movement from below' with the 'reforms from above'. Leftists must not reject the traditional strategy of seeking to win control of state institutions. But success here only makes sense if the state institutions are themselves under constant pressure from below – that is, if there are mass organizations capable of controlling their own leaders, and if necessary of forcing them to do what they would otherwise lack the willingness or resolution to do.

A turn to radical policies requires that left parties simultaneously carry through a social reorientation, and also demands a sort of moral revolution within them. Most organizations are incapable of coping with this dual upheaval, but this simply means that sooner or later they will finish up on the sidelines of history.

The Zapatistas

While socialist politicians are considering the limits of the possible, and discussing conformism and post-industrialism, spontaneous resistance to capitalist exploitation is taking on new forms. The revolt by the Indians in the Mexican province of Chiapas unexpectedly debunked the conceptions of the ideologues of the 'serious left' concerning what is possible and impossible in modern-day politics.

One eyewitness to the revolt in Chiapas dubbed it 'the end of "the end of history"'.[9] The rebels began an extensive armed struggle on 1 January 1994, capturing the town of San Cristobal. In the liberated zones they built amphitheatres, something like

Greek agoras and given the name *aguascalientes* in honour of the place where the assembly of popular representatives had been held during the Mexican revolution of 1914. European and Indian traditions, history and the modern world all converged in Chiapas. The authorities destroyed some of the *aguascalientes*, but not all. The movement's centre became the La Realidad base in the Lacandona jungle.

The insurgents called themselves the Zapatista National Liberation Army (EZLN) in memory of the hero of the Mexican revolution, General Zapata. The government responded with massive military operations, aerial bombardments and a propaganda war. But the rebels held the upper hand, and compelled the authorities to recognize them as a force that had to be reckoned with. Mexican President Ernesto Zedillo was obligied to hold talks with the Zapatistas despite his obvious and unconcealed wish to annihilate them.

The ideology of the Zapatistas amounted to an explicit rejection of 'vanguardism':

> Our form of struggle is not the only one; for many it may not even be an acceptable one. Other forms of struggle exist and have great value. Our organization is not the only one, for many it may not even be a desirable one. Other honest, progressive, and independent organizations exist and have great value. The Zapatista Army of National Liberation has never claimed that it is the only legitimate one. It's just the only one we were left. The EZLN salutes the honest and necessary development of all forms of struggle that will lead us to freedom, democracy and justice. The EZLN has never claimed its organization to be the only truthful, honest and revolutionary one in Mexico, or even in Chiapas. In fact, we organized ourselves this way because we were not left any other way.[10]

From this also flows the need for a complex, multi-level strategy.

> We think that revolutionary change in Mexico is not just a question of one kind of activity. It will come, strictly speaking, from neither an armed revolution or an unarmed one. It will be the result of struggles on several fronts, using a lot of

methods, various social forms, with different levels of commitment and participation. And the result will be not a triumph of a party, organization or alliance of organizations with their particular social programs, but rather the creation of a democratic space for resolving the confrontations between different political proposals.[11]

In the spirit of Rosa Luxemburg, Subcomandante Marcos recognized the advantages of spontaneity. Life in Chiapas taught the revolutionary intellectuals a great deal: 'One becomes spontaneous when living on the thin edge of war . . . .'[12] The revolutionary 'word' becomes not a prologue to the 'deed', but part of it, a reflection of revolutionary action. This new form of political utterance surprised and attracted people with the most diverse levels of education and of experience in politics and life. It proved effective against the most sophisticated forms of modern state propaganda, against the lies on television, against the advertising industry, and also against postmodernist 'discourse'.

The whole world was being told that socialism was dead.

But not everybody listens to the voices of hopelessness and resignation. Not everyone has jumped onto the bandwagon of despair. Most people continue on; they cannot hear the voice of the powerful and faint-hearted as they are defeated by the cry and the blood that death and misery should [sic] in their ears. But in moments of rest they hear another voice, not the one that comes from above, but rather the one that comes with the wind from below and is born in the heart of the indigenous people of the mountains, a voice that speaks of justice and liberty, a voice that speaks of socialism, a voice that speaks of hope . . . the only hope in this earthy world.[13]

The revolt by the Zapatistas was 'the first armed uprising against neo-liberalism' in history.[14] For this reason it immediately set up an enormous resonance throughout the whole world. In the summer of 1996 the Zapatistas held the First Intercontinental Meeting for Humanity and against Neoliberalism, which journalists described as 'one of the most unusual international conferences ever'. Marcos and his supporters were not in the least interested in founding some kind of new International. They mostly listened and observed. The participants were extremely diverse, ranging from revolutionary activists to film stars and intellectuals who had long ago forgotten the convictions of their youth. Nevertheless, the Zapatista leaders saw in this gathering a first step toward creating a 'collective network of all our particular struggles and resistances'.[15] At any rate, they succeeded in attracting world attention, which is essential for the internationalization of any movement.

The International Meeting in Chiapas confirmed that the Zapatista movement, even though it had arisen far from the centres of Western civilization, was not at all provincial or backward in the ideological and cultural sense. Zapatism appeared as a thoroughly convincing affirmation of the idea of communitarianism, which had gained currency among Western leftists in the mid-1990s. As the Mexican sociologist Adolfo Gilly writes:

> It is significant that it should be one of the oldest communitarian forms still in existence, that of the indigenous communities of the Mexican south-east, which has welcomed and supported one of the first, if not the first, form of radical rebellion of the end of this century. This form of rebellion places itself wholeheartedly on record not as supporting or opposing this or that, but as struggling against global neoliberalism. Instead of presenting a particular political line in counterposition to neoliberalism, it counterposes to it humanity, or if you like, the human condition.[16]

Meanwhile the events in Chiapas, like the other crises of the 1990s, have shown that communitarianism cannot take the place of a radical programme. It is significant that the ideas of communitarianism unite both left- and right-wing thinkers who defend the moral values of the community against the onslaught of neo-liberal capitalist practice, which depersonalizes and atomizes human beings. In such conditions the left naturally turns communitarian. However, it is not communitarianism but Marxism which allows us to develop concrete programmes of structural economic reforms, without which the appeals to community and solidarity remain empty declarations. Communitarianism can and must complement modern-day socialism, but it cannot replace it.

The problem faced by the Zapatista movement is that, while it provides a wonderful expression of the moods and hopes of the Indian south, it cannot achieve its goals unless it wins the support of the country's industrial north. The more fully it expresses the interests of the oppressed masses of Chiapas, the more difficulty it has in expanding its influence to other states. Meanwhile, only a broader programme of democratic and social demands will allow Zapatism to resolve this contradiction.

In essence, the heterogeneity of Mexican society provides a match for the heterogeneity of modern globalized capitalism. For the Zapatistas, however, this is a question not of sociological theory, but of practical politics. It is essential to transform the present set of concrete demands into 'the programme of a potential emerging social bloc'.[17] It is no simple task to unite urban industrial workers, specialists in post-industrial production, migrants, marginals, representatives of the informal sector and traditional Indian communities into a common movement, and then to coordinate their actions. Unless this task is accomplished, there will be neither victory nor even partial success. But modern capitalism itself is helping the left in this endeavour; capitalism in the course of its development gives rise, in quite natural fashion, to similar interests in all the above groups.

Zapatism, in the view of its supporters, acts as a unifying 'moral principle'. The readiness to act in the name of justice, without taking into account 'objective limitations' or the demands of '*Realpolitik*', transforms Zapatism into 'the regulative idea that makes it possible to distinguish the good from the bad, the just from the unjust, and the human from the inhuman'.[18] Morality and duty cannot in principle be based on criteria of success. Evil, when it triumphs, does not become good, and refusing to fulfil your duty does not cease to be a betrayal even if this is simpler and more convenient than fulfilling it. A society that proclaims success to be the supreme value cannot in principle be morally just. Counterposing its 'naive' idealism to the pragmatism of the 'official left', Zapatism has not only won a great moral victory, but has also restored a sense of purpose to the existence of the left movement as such.

The Zapatista movement has succeeded, in striking fashion, in combining in itself both traditionalism and innovativeness. The movement is not a repeat of the Latin American guerrilla movements of the 1960s, and neither is it a new edition of the revolutionary vanguard.

> The EZLN (Zapatista Army for National Liberation) is not – anymore or yet – a guerrilla movement (despite having started as one ten years ago after the elitist model of *foco*, the armed vanguard). It has become the organization of self-defence for some tens of thousands of excluded people – of three million inhabitants, Chiapas has a million indigenous people.[19]

Posing clear challenges to the principles of formal democracy, Zapatism at the same time has become a model of a profoundly democratic movement. The challenge to the state and the use of armed action were not a forced answer to the complete lack of interest by the authorities in their own citizens. The weakness of the institutions of formal democracy in the countries of the periphery and semi-periphery – or their purely decorative nature – has brought about a situation in which society's attitude to political violence has changed.

The Mexican elections of 1988, in which opposition candidate Cuauhtemoc Cardenas won a majority, but Carlos Salinas de Gortari became president instead, made the revolt in Chiapas inevitable. The theft of victory from the people changed the moral climate in society. To the most oppressed sectors of the population it became obvious that nothing could be expected from the state or from official society. To the radical sector of the left, it also became clear that the road to democracy and social justice would not lie through free elections, or at least, that these free elections would still have to be fought for. 'The fraudulent victory has delegitimized the ballot box in which they once had confidence, and they feel in the rebellion of the indigenous people a justified vengeance against their injuries and an echo of their own accumulated anger', writes the Mexican sociologist Adolfo Gilly.[20]

Cardenas's Party of the Democratic Revolution (PRD), which united a large section of the Mexican left, showed itself to be a principled but ineffective opposition. The more obvious its powerlessness in the face of the state apparatus, acting in close concert with local and foreign monopolies and the 'big brother' from the United States, the greater became the vacillations of its leaders. The erosion of mass support for Cardenism became an obvious fact, as did the demoralization of the activists and the desire of the parliamentary leaders to agree to a compromise with the authorities, who depended on corruption, on rigged elections, on the intimidation of the population and on the manipulation of public opinion. The general demoralization of the left that set in after 1989 could not fail to have an impact on the Mexican opposition as well. By the mid-1990s the opposition found itself in a strategic dead-end.

Despite the fact that Zapatism embodies the popular disillusionment with parliamentarism, it is not hostile either to parliamentary institutions as such, or to the parliamentary left.

> At different times and in different forms, Cardenism and Zapatism have represented identity symbols of the excluded sectors of the population, of the poor and oppressed. But neither Cardenism nor Zapatism will be able on its own to articulate the national opposition to this regime, an opposition expressed spontaneously in the diverse and multiple signs of revolt by the Mexican people. A convergence of respect and reciprocal tolerance will be necessary if resistance by Mexicans to the real powers and authorities – a multiple resistance by workers, by citizens, by human beings – is to be organized.[21]

Unfortunately the parliamentary left, a least on the public level, has shown much less sympathy for the Zapatistas than the Zapatistas have shown for the parliamentary left. This is due not only to fear by the latter that it will lose the role of sole representative of the opposition masses, but also to the uncomfortable pressure which the Zapatista movement has placed on leftists working within the framework of the parliamentary institutions and subject to their logic. But it is precisely this pressure that gives a real political point to work in these institutions, and which prevents this work from turning into pure fakery.

With the national state becoming more and more a tool of the bureaucracy and of transnational capital, while the traditional left opposition plays by the rules and reveals its total impotence, groups and leaders that are prepared to break the rules are becoming increasingly attractive. During the 1970s left radicals were seized by enthusiasm for a romantic cult of armed struggle, while the majority of workers were more and more placing their hopes on institutional reforms within the framework of democracy. In the 1990s, by contrast, former radicals are disowning 'terrorism', while a substantial part of society, disillusioned with the potential of representative organs and parliamentary politics, feels increasing sympathy for the people who are taking to arms. For hundreds of thousands of people in Chechnya, Latin America and Africa, 'criticism by the gun' has turned out to be not just the ultimate means of forcing the elites to take them into account, but the only means. The individuals involved here are not terrorists or guerrilla fighters of the 'traditional' type, attempting to seize territory and disorganize the authorities, or else simply venting their hatred of the system on particular representatives of the authorities. Nor are we dealing here with 1980s-style 'blind' terrorism, directed randomly against people who are not guilty of anything.

The armed actions are no longer aimed directly at the seizure of power. This is true even of movements that are achieving successes on the field of battle.[22] Subcomandante Marcos stresses that if real changes are to be forced in society, a 'civilian Zapatism' needs to arise alongside 'military Zapatism'. This has nothing in common with earlier strategies of creating a broad front around a 'vanguard' military-political organization.[23] 'Civilian Zapatism' has to acquire 'its own autonomy and organic life'. It has to become an equal partner of 'military Zapatism'.[24]

It is clear that a movement which is locked away in its 'base area' cannot be victorious unless it broadens its sphere of influence. Here we see the fundamental difference between Zapatism and previous insurgencies. If earlier insurgents sought primarily to broaden their zone of control and to extend their armed actions over as much territory as possible, the Zapatistas are trying to broaden their political influence. It is not essential for them to capture towns outside the borders of Chiapas, but they have to ensure that their demands are at the centre of national political debates. They have set out to collaborate with other political organizations and movements, to coordinate the efforts of the legal opposition with those of the insurgents, and the efforts of Indians in remote mountain regions with those of workers in modern cities. Issuing appeals to people throughout Mexico and all Latin America, they have not called specifically for a resort to arms, but have urged people to defend their rights in whatever way seems effective in each case.

Return to the Arms

Zapatistas were not the only guerrilla movement which was growing and increasing its political weight in the 1990s. Guerrillas belonging to the Revolutionary Armed Forces of Colombia (FARC) and National Liberation Army (ELN, also in Columbia) were gaining ground both militarily and politically. In 1998–99 their strength grew to such an extent that the Colombian authorities became really worried about the guerrillas approaching the capital, while the United States started discussing armed intervention. At the same time, some of the far left in Latin America accused FARC of being a 'wrong sort' of guerrilla movement, calling them 'armed reformists' because they tended to negotiate with the government, looking for a political solution to the civil war and calling for land reform and the expansion of the public sector instead of an immediate socialist revolution.[25]

In the mid-1980s a sort of 'new terrorism' made its appearance. Examples have included the actions of Shamil Basayev during the Chechen war, and the seizure of hostages in Peru in December 1996 by fighters from the Tupac Amaru Revolutionary Movement (MRTA) led by Nestor Cerpa Cartolini. The Moscow journal *Itogi* early in 1997 noted the similarities. The Peruvian guerrilla fighters, like the Chechens, had:

> a good grasp of the art of public relations, and in their actions began to orient themselves not so much toward a tangible result (ransom payments, the freeing of comrades and so on), as toward the propaganda effect. After seizing an embassy residence that occupied a whole block, they promptly set about disseminating a daily bulletin via the Internet, and organized an interview for world television through a press secretary in Hamburg. They even contrived to break a security forces blockade of the residence, and on 31 December held an improvised press conference, featuring their leader and the captured Japanese ambassador, for a group of foreign journalists. All this drove President Fujimori into a rage; as a result most of the officials responsible for anti-terrorist measures, including generals who had been taken hostage, were deprived of their posts.[26]

The Russian press noted that, unlike the Russian authorities, Fujimori in trying to resolve the crisis sought to keep his methods 'within civilized bounds'.[27] In reality, this was due solely to the identity of the hostages. The Peruvian guerrilla fighters seized representatives of the elite, ambassadors, ministers and generals, and, moreover, on the territory of a foreign embassy, while the Chechen insurgents took captive ordinary people whose lives in the view of the authorities were worth nothing. The Russian hostages, to the fury of the Moscow authorities and of the 'patriotic' press, did not hide their sympathy for the Chechen rebels who had seized them,[28] while the imprisoned Peruvian bureaucrats showed real class hatred for their captors. Throughout the whole time that the government was taking part in negotiations, security force units were preparing to storm the embassy residence, and were digging tunnels beneath the buildng. The authorities also managed to impose an information blockade on the fighters. It was this that was ultimately decisive. No longer able to communicate with the world, the rebels lost the political initiative as well. After a 127-day siege, the embassy residence was taken by storm, and all the rebels, including some who had surrendered and been taken prisoner, were killed. Nevertheless, this was a Pyrrhic victory for the Fujimori regime. Throughout the months of the siege the insurgent movement drew attention to itself and won new supporters; it proved, even at the cost of its leaders' lives, that it was capable not only of fighting, but also of conducting negotiations. As representatives of the MRTA declared, the insurgents would be forced to continue their search for peace simultaneously with their armed struggle, since the 'peaceful path' had been 'closed one more time'. Their campaign would seek to unite everyone who had 'seen in our struggle the revalidation of their own struggles, the hope of building a better world, without hunger, without unemployment, without neo-liberalism'.[29]

Violence has served as a means of influencing public opinion, of disorganizing the ruling-class propaganda machine, and of waking up civil society. Its goal has been to humiliate the authorities, to alter the logic of political behaviour in society and to show that the 'absolutely impossible' is becoming quite achievable. The seizing of hostages has been not so much a means of pressuring the authorities as a proof of their powerlessness, while the hostages themselves have been perceived not only as victims, but also as participants in the drama.

The armed struggle by the insurgents of the Guatemalan National Revolutionary Unity led ultimately to the reform of the legal system and of the armed forces, while putting an end to the suppression of Indian culture and to violations of human rights that had continued for many years. Without armed resistance these perfectly moderate reforms, which did not transgress the bounds of bourgeois democracy, would not have been implemented.

If the 'old' Latin American insurgent movements, which arose in the time of general enthusiasm for the ideas of Che Guevara, sought to become political parties, the Zapatistas, in the words of Marcos, are in no hurry to turn themselves into 'a traditional political force' like the Party of Revolutionary Democracy, or into a 'politico-military force'.[30] This is no accident. As scholars note, by the mid-1990s the majority of 'historic guerrilla' currents had been integrated into the dominant political system. As a result, their programmes and strategies now 'differ scarcely at all from the orientations of the reformist left'.[31] By contrast, the Zapatistas represent 'a new political culture'.[32] While using political and military means, they remain above all a movement. Their strength consists in the fact that they occupy an intermediate position between reformism and the revolutionary movement, between a political organization and a countercultural initiative, and between an insurgent army and a mass democratic union. If this movement is not isolated and ghettoized in the state of Chiapas, it could exert a decisive influence on the politics of the left, not just in Latin America but throughout the world. Marcos is not exaggerating when he speaks of an 'international Zapatism'.[33]

In the epoch of television and computers, the struggle will be waged not only in real space but also in virtual space. Here the traditional leftists have proven totally powerless. The insurgents, on the other hand, have managed to change this. The seizing of hostages and other armed actions created a quite new information situation. It has become impossible simply to remain silent about events, as was done in the totalitarian propaganda of the Soviet period. The market constantly demands new and variegated information. But in political terms, lying is now going unpunished; even if lies are refuted within a few weeks or even days, this no longer matters, since social consciousness will by this time be occupied with other, fresher subjects. The memory of the television viewer is constantly being washed away, and his or her attention dissipated; the past is losing all meaning.

The tactics of Basayev, of Nestor Cerpa Cartolini and, to a significant degree, of Marcos as well, consisted of shifting the struggle onto the territory of the enemy, and of undermining the hegemony of the ruling groups in the virtual space. Through their actions in the real world, the rebel leaders paralysed the machine of virtual propaganda. Their actions were not only armed agitation. Events developed in such a way that lying on television became counterproductive and even impossible. Each lie was refuted by the further course of events, not in a few days or weeks, but within a few hours, before people had yet managed to forget it. In addition, it became advantageous to tell the truth. The truth was spectacular and meaningful, while the lies were dismal and senseless. The short-term commercial interests of the television companies were in conflict with their social calling. The information front of the authorities was pierced.

At the same time as leftists throughout the world were lamenting the hostility of the mass media, the Zapatistas set out to force the press and television to work for them, despite the ideology that dominated those industries. The leader of the insurgency became popular throughout the world. 'Guerrilla fighter or superstar?' Régis Debray wrote of Marcos: 'Neither one nor the other. A creative activist.' Marcos, Debray observed, used publicity 'not as an aim, but a means. For him media action is Clausewitz's war applied to newspapers: the political extended by other means.'[34]

Protests and Programmes

The ideological collapse of socialism in the early 1990s could not put an end to popular protests. The mass outpourings were sparked not by agitation, and not by ideology, but by social and national oppression, by people's miserable situation. Amid the ideological crisis of the left, however, the programmes of mass popular movements became obscure and ill-defined. When people took up arms, they were clearly conscious of what they were fighting against, but it was much harder for them to formulate what they were fighting for.

When a mass uprising against the dictator Mobutu seized Zaire late in 1996, the front ranks of the rebel forces included activists from Marxist revolutionary organizations. The majority of them, however, had already lost sight of their clear ideological reference-points of earlier days. 'Some openly call for socialism, but others do not, as is often the case in the Third World today.'[35] There was no clear programme and the unity was based on a shared hatred of the Mobutu regime. Not surprisingly, the new regime failed to meet people's expectations and the victors soon started fighting against each other.

The political programme of Shamil Basayev, 'a spontaneous Chechen socialist', as the Moscow press described him, could be reduced to the simplest of principles: 'I don't want Chechnya to have 3 per cent of super-rich people who oppress all the rest.'[36] Victory in the war, however, confronted the former fighters with a difficult problem: how to bring their principles to fruition in the conditions of peace. The peace revealed how confused and inconsistent were political and economic ideas of the winners. With socialist ideas being discredited and no reformist programmes developed, Chechen radicals turned to Islam.

The free territory of Chechnya is not a model of a new state, but a self-regulating society. Its spiritual energy feeds on the experience and traditions of the past, but not on an ideal of the future. This is the source both of the movement's strength and of its weakness. The journalist Galina Kovalskaya, who brilliantly described the life of the Chechen resistance fighters, noted that for the insurgents the counterbalance to the Russian 'arbitrariness' was a desire to live 'according to the rules', or at least to seem to do so.[37] These rules were not taken from the laws of Islam; they developed spontaneously, combining the customs of the mountain people, Soviet discipline and Muslim morality. When the rebel army, two-thirds of which was made up of mountain peasants, defeated elite Russian units and freed the Chechen capital, Grozny, the system of norms collapsed. Everything was heaped unexpectedly on the victors – a large city instead of mountain villages, peace instead of war, the task of constructing a state instead of organizing defence. Confusion and fragmentation dominated political life of free Chechnya after the war. Hope turned into frustration and freedom into chaos.

It is possible to attain victory even without a programme or an ideology. But it is far more difficult to make use of the fruits of your victory. The fact that insurgent movements are shunning the temptations of a dogmatic 'simplicity', and are taking up the difficult search for concrete answers to specific problems, is a huge step forward compared to the times of ready-made 'models'. But ideological reference-points are still necessary. Neither democratic principles, nor 'social Islam', nor the principle of 'honest power' are sufficient in ideological terms to transform protest into creation. 'The intensifying anger of the people must be channelled through organised political forces', says a declaration of the Indonesian People's Democratic Party.[38] In essence, any serious left movement can inscribe this on its banners.

Rifondazione in Italy

Although Subcomandante Marcos has showed that it is possible to carry on theoretical work in any circumstances, it is hard to develop a concept of a social alternative while you are under fire from the enemy. This is why, despite the huge significance of the new insurgent movements, a great deal depends on the institutionalized left parties of the 'new wave'.

As a rule, such organizations arise and develop most rapidly where influential workers' parties of the traditional type have either been absent, or failed to survive the shocks of the years from 1989 to 1991. Parties to the left of social democracy exist and have real influence in most countries of the European Union. The question is not only how radical these parties are but also whether they represent a political alternative.

The disappearance of the Communist Party of Italy was accompanied not only by the appearance in its place of the impotent and conciliationist Party of the Democratic Left. The self-liquidation of Italian communism occurred in slow, agonizing fashion. Achille Ochetto, who between 1989 and 1991 began gradually transforming the Communist Party into something whose character was quite unknown (at first it did not even have a name), promised to create:

a new political formation, democratic, popular, reformist, open to various progressive tendencies both secular and Catholic, capable of formulating new demands, arising out of the worlds of labour and culture as well as from among the youth and women's movements, environmentalists, pacifists, the movement against violence, and feminism.[39]

In reality the new organization 'united' only the structures of the Communist Party, and not even fully at that. The only leftists to take part in the unification process were the members of the small Trotskyist group *Socialismo Rivoluzionario*, and before long they too finished up on the sidelines. Instead of a new force for reform, what emerged was an amorphous political group with neither ideology, strategy, clear goals or its own culture. Ochetto did not manage to hold onto the post of leader. The Party of the Democratic Left was headed by the new leader D'Alema, who directed it still further to the right. But meanwhile, *Rifondazione Communista* appeared on the political scene. This was a new party defending the old tradition.

Rifondazione is a unique coalition of diverse currents. Here there are nostalgic communists, united around Armando Cossutta; Eurocommunists who remain true to the ideas of Enrico Berlinguer, who headed the Communist Party in the 1970s; supporters of his constant intra-party left critic Pietro Ingrao; Trotskyists from the former *Democrazia Proletaria* party; and neo-Marxists from the *Il Manifesto* group. These elements are united mainly by hostility to the conciliationist policies of the 'official' left. However, this has been enough for Rifondazione to emerge as a substantial force in the country's political life.

In essence, Rifondazione (which later called itself the Party of Communist Refoundation – PRC) has become the type of organization that the Party of the Democratic Left pledged to become but did not: a broad union of reformist, alternative and revolutionary currents. Rifondazione is strongest in the traditional zones of communist influence, and in the course of the 1990s its popularity has steadily risen. After the coming to power of the 'progressive' Prodi government the leadership of Rifondazione was faced with a difficult choice: whether to support Prodi, who did not conceal his intention of pursuing a neo-liberal course in 'left' packaging, or to refuse to support him, and thus to play into the hands of right-wing populists who were waiting for their time to come. Rifondazione decided in favour of giving critical support to the Prodi government, but did not accept cabinet positions. However, the practical measures taken by the government have shocked even supporters of Rifondazione who did not expect anything good from the new authorities. As a result the party has finished up in bitter conflict with its 'partners' in the parliamentary majority.

If Rifondazione has not been able to halt the march of the left majority to the right, it has at least managed to preserve its reputation as a principled force and to lay the basis for forming a serious left alternative in the future. However, the price has been high. Angry debates have raged within the party over its relations with the left government. A number of deputies have left the party, accusing it of excessive radicalism, and have set up their own Movement of United Communists, which has in practice become a satellite of the Party of the Democratic Left. At the same time, Rifondazione activists have criticized the leaders for showing insufficient firmness in relation to a government, which is in practice implementing neo-liberal policies. In October 1998 the government crisis erupted again. This time it was Armando Cossutta and the supporters of Stalinist traditions who voted for Prodi, even though the majority of Rifondazione members supported the party leader Fausto Bertinotti who declared no confidence in the government.

A considerable number of Rifondazione deputies supported Cossutta against the rank-and-file members. That did not save the government which had to resign. But it caused a split in Rifondazione. A new party was formed by the deserters – the Party of the Italian Communists. Its leaders were immediately rewarded by posts in the new government of ex-communist D'Alema. Neo-liberal policies with a leftist face were given another chance.

The division between the rightward-drifting 'political class' and the radicalizing masses has thus been reproduced within the left party, which set out to overcome this split.

Party of Democratic Socialism in Germany

In the course of the unification of Germany, the eastern *Länder* gave birth to another political organization that has thrown down a challenge both to social democracy and to old-style communism. Before the crisis of 1989 the Socialist Unity Party of Germany (SED), that held power in the German Democratic

Republic, had been one of the most orthodox in Eastern Europe. Reformist currents existed within it, but they were neither particularly visible nor organized. At the same time, the general situation in the GDR meant that, to a much greater degree than in the other 'fraternal countries', the reformers based their position not only on the desire for greater economic efficiency, but also on the need to realize the potential of socialism. During the GDR's last years one of the leaders of the reformist wing of the SED was the party secretary in Saxony, Hans Modrow.

An extraordinary congress of the Socialist Unity Party of Germany in December 1989 resolved to transform it into the Party of Democratic Socialism (PDS), a modern, pluralist left party combining 'social democratic, socialist, communist, anti-fascist and pacifist traditions'.[40] This was preceded by a thoroughgoing revolt of the party rank and file, who demanded the replacement of the old leadership and the reorienting of the party. Nothing of the kind occurred either in the Soviet Union, nor in other countries of Eastern Europe. This revolt was part of the general democratic movement that swept eastern Germany in the autumn of 1989 and which provided, as was argued at the conference, a chance for the 'radical renewal and reform [*radikale Neuformierung*]' of the party.[41]

At the extraordinary congress, 41-year-old lawyer Gregor Gysi was elected chairperson of the party. In the era of the GDR Gysi had acted as defence counsel in the trials of dissidents who included the distinguished Marxist Rudolf Bahro. An energetic and charismatic leader, who loved of jokes and paradoxes, Gysi was completely unlike the dull social-democratic leaders and old party *apparatchiks*. In February 1990 a second session of the congress was held, and a new programme and statutes were adopted. Heated discussion erupted between people who demanded that the old party be dissolved and a new one founded, and others who insisted on maintaining continuity. The victory of the latter made it possible to retain part of the traditional membership base and property, but at the same time guaranteed that the PDS would inherit a mass of problems and the label 'successor to the Stalinist SED'. Initially, the party even kept the dual name SED-PDS, though it renounced this as soon as the bureaucratic process of formalizing the succession had been completed. The material base which the PDS inherited from the old state party was very modest. After unification, when the new authorities confiscated all the buildings and funds that had been handed over to the party during the years of the GDR, the PDS retained only a few buildings that had belonged to the communists before the coming to power of the Nazis.

Although the PDS differed little in its origins from other post-communist parties, its political trajectory turned out to be quite different. The reasons need to be sought in the peculiarities of the situation that existed in eastern Germany following the unification. Here the old *nomenklatura* was not only unable to head the process of capitalist counter-revolution, but could not even participate in it. The Western bourgeoisie did not give it a chance. In exactly the same way, the existence of a genuine, strong social democracy in the 'old *Länder*' made impossible the emergence of another social democratic party in the east. The 'social democratic platform' in the PDS did not manage to play a substantial role. A post-communist party could survive only by acting as a radical alternative and, at the same time, by decisively taking its distance from the Stalinist past. This was understood even by party activists who in other circumstances would perhaps have spoken out in support of a more moderate course. The radical renovators succeeded with relative ease in winning a majority in the leadership and in beginning a unique political experiment – building a left socialist party of the 'new generation' on the ruins of one of the most orthodox of all Stalinist organizations.

The collapse of the communist system in East Germany was accompanied by a powerful mass outburst of democratic energy, felt not only on the streets and squares, but also in the workplaces. The subsequent experience of unification meant that this energy did not have a chance to become embodied in the concrete activity of carrying out changes, and the PDS was almost the only political channel into which it could be directed.

Analysing the history of workers' councils in the former GDR, the radical Berlin journal *Sklaven*, which has taken an extremely critical attitude to the PDS, notes that despite a 'conflict between grass-roots democratic and apparatus leftists', this party has been the only political force that has 'given the workers' movement organizational, financial and propaganda support'. As a result, the party's activity in the workplaces can be characterized as 'out-standingly successful'.[42] It does not by any means follow that the priorities of the PDS leaders have always coincided with those of the party activists. Rather, the opposite has been true; contradictions between the two have arisen constantly. But the party's ability to collaborate with people and groups holding more radical positions has been an obvious advantage it has possessed compared with the social democratic and trade union bureaucracies of the West.

In the last elections to the *Volkskammer* (parliament) of the GDR on 18 March 1990, the PDS scored impressive results, especially in traditional working-class districts. The overall victors, however, were the Christian Democrats, who promised general prosperity following a rapid unification. The government headed by PDS member Hans Modrow resigned. Power in East Berlin was taken by a Christian Democratic government headed by Lothar de Maizere, later revealed to be a former agent of the GDR's state security organization.

The elections for the first united Bundestag in 1992, brought more results for the PDS. The party received 2.4 per cent of the votes (11.1 per cent in the east and 0.3 per cent in the west). It gained representation in the parliament thanks only to a special rule that ensured special quotas for 'eastern' parties. In the elections of 1994 support for the PDS almost doubled, with the party receiving 4.4 per cent of the votes throughout Germany as a whole. Despite failing to reach the barrier of 5 per cent, the PDS was again represented in the Bundestag; because it won four direct mandates from territorial districts, the votes received by its list were taken into account. An important element in the PDS's electoral strategy was its 'open lists', that included representatives of the 'left spectrum' who were not required to have 'direct or indirect links with the party'. Non-members of the PDS made up 13 per cent of the deputies who were elected on these lists in the eastern *Länder*.[43] In all, the PDS and its allies had 30 deputies in the 1994 Bundestag. The party was represented in all the Landtage (regional parliaments) and municipal assemblies in the eastern *Länder*, where it was the third and in some cases second largest force.

After Gregor Gysi became the head of the party's Bundestag fraction, he quit his post as party leader, and the PDS came to be headed by Lothar Bisky. The party still encountered a multitude of problems, from the exposure of former GDR state security agents in its ranks, to attacks by the authorities of the new Germany. It was also wracked by internal disagreements.

The collapse of the GDR confronted democratic socialists with serious problems, but ultimately predetermined the metamorphosis of the PDS into one of the outstanding left parties of the new wave, a party unique in Western Europe. The uniqueness of the PDS consists above all in the fact that it is the only party in the West that directly represents the interests of the periphery. This stems from the position of Germany's eastern *Länder*, which on the one hand are part of the most powerful capitalist country in Europe, and on the other, as PDS theoreticians explain, represent its 'economic and social periphery'.[44] This is also the source of the party's policy of trying to represent both social and regional interests. At first many leaders of the party saw the continuing division of the country into western and eastern (corresponding to 'old' and 'new') *Länder* as something temporary. 'As a socialist party, a left alternative, we cannot remain a regional party for long. The East German identity will disappear in the next five to eight years', said André Brie.[45] Subsequent developments have shown, however, that everything is far more complex. The existence of the periphery is predetermined by the very nature of the capitalist economy. The eastern identity has persisted because specific 'eastern' problems have remained. They have changed as well, but with every new cycle of the market this contradiction has been reproduced in a new form.

Public opinion surveys conducted in 1997 have shown that nostalgia for the GDR is dying out, but that the differences between Ossies and Wessies remain. As before, the characteristic desire of eastern Germans is for social justice, combined with an equally distant attitude ('*Wieder-noch-Haltungen*') toward the old GDR and the new FRG.[46] Sociologists have noted that the overwhelming majority of the population of the eastern *Länder*, including those who do not vote for the left, are 'unconscious socialists'.[47]

In the present situation regionalism does not in any way contradict the ideology or strategic perspectives of the socialist movement. As one of the documents of the PDS states, the party is not 'eastern', but 'a socialist party that came from the east' (*aus dem Osten kam*).[48] The problem does not lie in abandoning regionalism, but in the question of how to combine it with a broader strategy – not only all-German, but also all-European. 'Without a breakthrough to the East, there will not be a breakthrough to the West!', the PDS documents proclaim. The eastern

Germans have to 'go on the offensive in order to bring about changes' in Germany as a whole.[49]

The years 1996 and 1997 saw a new strengthening of the PDS, this time through an influx of activists and supporters in the West. Here the party remained an insignificant minority, but its rate of growth was striking. Hanover became the first large city in the 'old *Länder*' where the PDS succeeded in winning positions in local government organs (prior to this there were only cases in which dissatisfied municipal councillors from the 'Greens' crossed over to the PDS). Elections in Marburg yielded a sensational result; here 6.2 per cent of voters backed the PDS list, and the party received four places in the city assembly. An old university centre, Marburg is a traditional bastion of the left, where even in Cold War years the communists were strong. However, the party of Gregor Gysi and Lothar Bisky strengthened its positions in other large cities as well.[50]

In the 1998 parliamentary election, the PDS won half a million new votes, broke through the 5 per cent barrier and re-entered the Bundestag with a group of 35 deputies. It was the only party in Germany besides the triumphant Social Democrats to gain votes. A month later, after an impressive electoral victory in the East German province of Mecklenburg-Vorpommern, the PDS for the first time entered provincial government. And in the 1999 European elections the party won 5.8 per cent of the votes and for the first time entered the European parliament.

In western Germany it was young members of the intelligentsia who were most receptive to the ideas of the PDS, and the party's influence spread from university cities. In the east the main concentrations of PDS voters were in large industrial centres, but more than half of the supporters of Gysi and Bisky lived outside the party's traditional strongholds.

Despite the appearance of new members in the western *Länder*, the PDS remained, at least in the east, a party of elderly people, who made up 67 per cent of its members. While the PDS was increasingly popular among the young voters, the membership base that had been inherited from the SED was growing old and dying. The only consolation for the socialist leaders was the fact that 'the same was happening to other parties as well'.[51]

During the period from 1990 to 1994, when the party's very survival was in question, the slogan of the PDS became the creation, in the words of writer and former GDR dissident Stefan

Heym, of 'a strong, authentic left opposition'.[52] The situation changed after the victories by the party in 1994 and 1995. Not only had democratic socialists almost doubled the number of their supporters, but they held power in many small urban centres, and in the land of Sachsen-Anhalt the PDS fraction held the fate of the government in its hands. On certain conditions, the leftists had agreed to 'tolerate' (*tolerieren*) a social democratic administration. This not only gave the PDS a de facto right of veto, but also forced the social democrats to coordinate their policies with the opposition.

It is not surprising that alongside the slogan of 'opposition', the new word 'responsibility' has appeared in the lexicon of the PDS. Magdeburg, the capital of Sachsen-Anhalt, became a sort of testing-ground where mechanisms were worked out, and where the possibilities, limitations and problems of the new reformism were revealed.

The actions of the PDS in Magdeburg provoked a bitter polemic within the party. Supporters of Ernest Mandel from the Union for Socialist Politics (VSP) who had joined the party observed that the success in Magdeburg was fraught with the danger of 'adaptation by the PDS to the capitalist system'.[53] Representatives of the Communist Platform and of the party's youth section spoke out still more sharply against the Magdeburg experiment. In parallel with the ideological criticism, conducted under the slogan 'Our place is in opposition!', a serious discussion also began on the theme of the acceptability and limits of political compromises.

The dissatisfaction of the party's left wing had a real basis. While outlining unquestionable achievements in the sphere of social policy, Petra Sitte, the chairperson of the PDS fraction in the Sachsen-Anhalt Landtag, also acknowledged that during the 'Magdeburg experiment' her fraction had become more differentiated, and that the earlier openness in the taking of decisions had disappeared. For this, however, she blamed the social democrats, who were refusing to discuss publicly questions of the budget and of regional policy. 'The more intensive our collaboration, the more difficult it is to apply the principle of openness.'[54]

The ideologue of the 'Magdeburg experiment' Roland Claus, on whom the fire of the left wing of the PDS was concentrated, argued that radical criticism of the system was ineffective unless it was complemented by a concrete reformist project. The 'Magdeburg experiment', he maintained, was providing a chance to formulate such a project on the basis of real practice. 'But there are no chances without risks. If we want real reforms, we have to meet these risks half-way.'[55]

The real test for the 'Magdeburg experiment' was the election of the new Landtag in April 1998. Paradoxically, PDS was both rewarded and punished for its policies. On the one hand, PDS picked up 20 per cent of the vote and came close to doing better than Chancellor Helmut Kohl's Christian Democrats. While the vote of Christian Democrats collapsed, Social Democrats improved their score by mere 2 per cent. Free democrats (liberals) and right-wing Greens (who were famous for their animosity towards PDS) failed to get the 5 per cent necessary to enter the parliament. The influence of PDS in local politics increased dramatically. The 'Magdeburg model' began to spread. In Meklenburg-Vorpommern, after the 1998 election, the PDS not only held the balance of power but formed a ruling coalition together with Social Democrats.

On the other hand, in the context of growing dissatisfaction with the reality of 'united Germany', the PDS this time proved to be unable to attract most of protest vote as it had earlier. A neo-Nazi German People's Union (DVU) won 13 per cent of the vote and became the fourth biggest party in Sachsen-Anhalt. Almost one-third of voters under the age of 30 cast their votes for the DVU. Many of them were just confused jobless young people who could be won for the cause of the left.

A second burning question for the PDS has remained the party's attitude to the GDR, to the SED and to the communist tradition in general. Unlike the situation in the countries of Central and Eastern Europe, where the party *nomenklaturas* effortlessly changed their ideology while retaining the old structures, what was involved in eastern Germany was the complex spiritual evolution of hundreds of thousands of rank and file party members, who in re-evaluating their experience tried not simply to condemn the past, but also to find in it a basis on which to mount a struggle for the future. The PDS was pursuing a course directly opposite to that of the other post-communist parties. Without denying the continuity of ideological tradition, the party set about radically changing its structures, forms and methods of work. In this sense, the PDS can be considered a spontaneously arising example of innovative neo-traditionalism.

On the one hand, it is constantly stressed that 'the PDS does not consider itself a communist party'.[56] Moreover, some of its best-known members are determined anti-communists. On the other hand, the various elements of the party include the 'communist platform' group. Party theoreticians try to reconcile these tendencies by referring to tradition and to the views of communist dissidents in the GDR (key names here are those of Robert Havemann, Ernst Bloch and Bertolt Brecht), and also by calling for a 'critical definition of our relationship to the original communist ideology'.[57]

In reality, the party's relationship to communist ideology has by no means been its key problem. An opposition force in the new united Germany and at the same time an organization of people who held reformist positions in the old GDR, the PDS has had to find its own identity, defending its principles while at the same time displaying pragmatism and seriousness in carrying out concrete tasks. Wolfram Adolphi, the editor of the journal *Utopie-Kreativ*, which is close to the party, speaks of the paradoxical union of the experience of eastern communist reformism and of the extra-parliamentary opposition of the 1960s and 1970s in the old West Germany. On this basis a new concept of political realism has appeared, something quite different from what has been seen among the social democratic and post-communist activists of recent years. Early in the century Rosa Luxemburg spoke of 'revolutionary Realpolitik'.[58] For the PDS this is becoming a formula for survival. Adolphi considers the marks of realism to be a determined readiness to go out and 'confront the unknown', to 'break with routine' and not to fear the 'constant presence of the unusual'.[59]

The constant struggle between currents and groups often causes irritation within the party. Many participants in the discussion recognize that ideological disputes are becoming an end in themselves, and that serious discussion of strategy and tactics is being replaced by 'pseudo-debates' (*Scheindebatten*). Party chairperson Lothar Bisky has even stated: 'We must not blockade one another, while we are all waging a common fight against a political blockade.'[60]

However, the party discussions have merely grown broader, and have grown along with the strength of the party and the spread of its influence. The constant disagreements within the PDS reflect not only the weaknesses of its left strategy, but also the heterogeneity of the party's social base. The same organization contains people from the eastern and western *Länder* (Ossies and Wessies), Germans and immigrants (including Turks and Kurds), radical youth and left-conservative pensioners, industrial workers and people involved with new technologies, technocrats and intellectuals, and, last but not least, men and women.

After the Social Democratic victory of 1998 a Red-Green government was formed by Gerhard Schroeder. That created both new opportunities and new strategic dilemmas for the PDS. The party spoke about pushing the government to the left while the government in practice was moving to the right. Oskar Lafontaine, the leader of the left within the German Social Democratic party resigned, the Red-Green government led the country into the war against Serbia. Leftist activists and voters who supported the Greens in the election were appalled. 'What's to be done, when a red-green government supports an illegal war?', wrote Elmar Altvater, one of the founders and ideologues of the Green Party. 'A conservative government wouldn't have been worse.'[61] Some members of the Greens and Social Democrats deserted to PDS as the only party opposing the war. All that forced the PDS to adopt a tougher approach towards social democracy. And this radicalism was rewarded by the growing number of members and voters in 1999.

While the voters were becoming more and more dissatisfied with the Social Democrats, the electoral strength of the PDS continued to increase. In autumn 1999 the Social Democrats were defeated in provincial elections in their traditional strongholds – Saarland, Brandenburg and Thuringia – and crushed in conservative Saxony. In Brandenburg, the PDS came close to the SPD, in Thuringia and Saxony the PDS won more votes than the Social Democrats, becoming the second biggest party in these two provinces and, possibly, in East Germany as a whole. In the West, too, the PDS made inroads, getting its supporters elected to communal bodies in a number of provinces.

The PDS formulates its role in German politics as 'democratic, social and ecological opposition from the left'.[62] And it plays this role quite successfully. The question remains how proceed from opposing the system to structural change.

The Workers' Party in Brazil

The Brazilian Workers' Party (PT) also belongs to the category of 'recently established' and 'politically heterogeneous' organizations. 'The growing strength of the *Partido dos Trabalhadores* on the Brazilian political scene does not represent the continuation of a long process of growth on the part of the Brazilian left. On the contrary, it stems from a "privilege of lateness"', wrote the Brazilian sociologist Emir Sader and the American journalist Ken Silverstein in a book devoted to the rise of the PT:

> When the party began organizing in 1979, almost a decade had passed since the country's historically weak left had been wiped out by the military regime of 1964 to 1985. The Brazilian Communist Party, outlawed but operating clandestinely since 1947, had lost expression even earlier, soon after the coup itself.[63]

Unlike the populist and sectarian revolutionary left, the Workers' Party took shape as a mass workers' organization, closely linked to the trade unions and to the new social movements. The ideological heterogeneity of the PT is striking; it includes various Marxist currents, adherents of liberation theology, and social democrats. The party's stronghold is São Paulo, the country's most modern and industrialized city, with a highly qualified workforce and post-industrial technologies. At the same time, the PT has also won mass support in the countryside, among landless peasants often living in semi-feudal conditions.

In the presidential elections of 17 December 1989 the PT's candidate, Luis Ignacio 'Lula' da Silva, lost by only 5 per cent to the candidate of the right, Fernando Collor. The PT's success in the elections of 1989, and Collor's extremely unsuccessful administration, which was accompanied by scandals and which ended with his premature resignation, created near-certainty among PT activists that Lula would become the next president of Brazil. In public opinion surveys in 1993, he outstripped likely rivals by 20 per cent. But the leftists gravely underestimated the power of the Brazilian bourgeoisie. The country's next president was not Lula, but Fernando Henrique Cardoso, a former radical sociologist.

The Brazilian ruling circles were forced to choose the most 'left-wing' candidate they could find. Cordoso's Marxist past disoriented substantial numbers of PT activists, who held out hopes of collaborating with the new administration. Moreover, the PT, like any large workers' party that becomes involved in government on the local level, by this time contained an influential right wing calling for the 'social democratization' of the Brazilian left. Following the defeat in the 1994 elections, a number of parliamentary leaders of the left dreamed of collaborating with the 'progressive' President Cardoso. These illusions, however, were not fated to last. On becoming president, the former Marxist began implementing harsh neo-liberal policies, which ultimately ruled out any possibility of collaboration.[64]

As PT activists admitted, the election defeat of 1994 revealed a 'strategic vacuum'.[65] Before the elections, too much weight had been placed on the candidacy of Lula, in hopes of a quick conquest of the central power. But the party also possessed a different type of experience, which allowed it to survive electoral failure and quickly to restore its influence as the country's leading political force.

The PT's most important achievement during the 1990s has been its active work in local self-government. The four years during which the left held power in the country's largest city, São Paulo, were not a staggering success, though there is no cause to speak of failure either. The PT local administration implemented a policy of municipalizing transport, while constantly stressing the difference between its methods and traditional 'statization'. On certain conditions, private enterprises were also brought within the public sector. The main goal of municipalization was to establish a 'social tariff for public transport'.[66]

Despite an energetic beginning, the left administration in São Paulo was unable to consolidate its social base and hold on to power. To a significant degree this was linked with the growing influence within its ranks of 'realism', which led ultimately to a bitter confrontation with the municipal services unions. The latter were disappointed with the results of the work of the left-wing mayor's office.

The PT's achievements have been much greater in Porto Alegre and Belo Horizonte. Cities with populations of several hundred thousand, and in some cases of more than a million, have been under the party's administration. Municipal resources are being used to implement active investment policies, allowing the creation of jobs, and the principle of openness and public accountability has been affirmed in the making of decisions. Public property is not administered by anonymous bureaucrats, but by the public itself on the basis of a 'participative budget', the formulating of which begins on the level of local citizens' assemblies.[67] In the words of PT ideologues, the point of this policy is 'the winning of civil rights on the level of the city'.[68]

The municipal elections of 1996 were a test of the party's ability to survive the defeat it suffered in the battle for the presidency. These elections revealed a broadening of the party's social base and of its geographical zone of influence. In the large industrial centres that form the PT's traditional base, it received somewhat fewer votes than in the presidential elections, but it dramatically strengthened its presence in the relatively undeveloped regions of the north, where it had earlier been weak. The main reason it lost votes in the south was not administrative problems in the cities where the party held power (surveys showed that the population was satisfied), but constant public disagreements between various tendencies. Where the leftists managed to act as a united force, they achieved successes.

The fears of moderate party leaders who considered that radical local activists would implement 'an excessively narrow policy of alliances' were not borne out.[69] In the final accounting, the more radical local organizations won greater support from voters than the moderate ones.

Struggles in Eastern Europe

The left in Eastern Europe remains weak, divided and overshadowed by the presence of the fake left, represented either by liberal social democratic parties or by the 'communist' parties which replaced the ideology of socialism with nationalism and anti-semitism. It is also suffering because of its inability to develop strategies and organizations adequate to the new reality of peripherical capitalism they are facing.

During the 1990s, in different countries there were attempts to establish a political force to the left of social democracy or at least a 'genuine' social democratic party. In Poland the Union of Labour achieved some degree of success, but failed to present a clear alternative to neo-liberalism. In the 1997 elections it lost almost half of its vote and all its parliamentary seats. In Hungary the Left Platform was formed inside the Socialist Party. The left expressed doubts about privatization, though not rejecting it completely, and called for the policies that could 'moderate the social burdens falling on the population'.[70] Criticizing the party's neo-liberal orientation, the Left Platform nevertheless remained within its ranks, unable to become an independent force. Leftist currents emerged in most of the post-communist parties but in almost every case they failed to break decisively with leaders who carried out neo-liberal policies. For the majority of people outside organized politics the differences between the leadership and the left currents remained unclear, if not unknown.

In the Czech Republic all attempts to create a new leftist organization failed. The resurrected Social Democratic Party was clearly right wing and the Communist Party, which retained a considerable strength remained dogmatic and nostalgic. The tradition of 1968 Marxist reformism seemed to disappear completely from political life.

In the Ukraine the Socialist Party was formed in 1991–92 with a very radical programme. Its leader, Oleksandr Moroz, was elected speaker of the Ukrainian parliament in 1994 and became one of the most popular political figures in the country. In 1998 the Socialists running in coalition with the Peasants' Party won 9.38 per cent of the vote and 35 seats.[71] However, that success was accompanied by a steady move to the right. Ivan Chizh, the leader of the Socialist fraction in the parliament insists that 'the Ukrainian socialists will always be more left wing than European ones'.[72] But that was reflected only in theoretical debates about the nature of socialism, not in politics. To make things worse, even those who represented the 'radical wing' of the party looked for inspiration not to Marxism or even Keynesianism but to different postmodern fashions. In 1997 the ideologue of the Socialist Party, Volodimir Kizima, wrote about 'libertarian alternative' to capitalism.[73] The party also was gradually absorbing the ideology of Ukrainian nationalism.[74] Discontented left-wing socialists split away and formed the Progressive Socialist Party that entered parliament in 1998 with 4.4 per cent of votes and 17 seats. The PSP remained weak and sectarian, however, seeing itself as the only 'genuine' left in the country.

It was the Communist Party of the Ukraine, resurrected after the 1991 collapse, that became in 1998 the leading left-wing force with 27 per cent of vote and 123 seats. The party lacked a clear programme, was confused in its attitude towards the Soviet past and remained stuck exactly half-way between hard-line Stalinism and reformist Eurocommunism. The same can be said of the two rival communist parties in Belarus. Divided over their attitude towards president Aleksandr Lukashenko, these two parties are engaged in a bitter struggle between themselves, rarely discussing strategic or theoretical issues. The enemies of Lukashenko point to his authoritarian inclinations while his supporters stress the social and economic achievements of the republic which rejected IMF-backed neo-liberal reforms and privatization, and kept most of its welfare state intact.[75]

In Russia all the new leftist parties that emerged after 1991 were defeated in 1993–94. The Party of Labour attempted to unite the radical intelligentsia with the trade union movement. This formation absorbed a large proportion of the active membership of the informal groups, which were very important during Gorbachev's rule. The Party of Labour was a typical pluralist organization, including social democratic, Marxist and even anarcho-syndicalist currents. However, it remained a relatively narrow club of socialist intellectuals and trade union activists, lacking a mass base. The workers' movement was in decline and the party clearly lacked resources for reaching out to the masses. The spontaneous resistance to neo-liberal reforms was more successfully organized by radical communist groups hoping for the return of the good old Soviet times. The Party of Labour finally collapsed after the coup launched by president Yeltsin in 1993, when trade union leaders, fearing reprisals from the government, withdrew all their support from the party and even purged radicals from their structures.

The Socialist Party of Workers (SPT) also formed in 1991–92, in its early period enjoyed an important strategic advantage, since it was able to act as a sort of bridge between the moderate wing of the communists and the non-communist left. The SPT also possessed certain material resources and was for a short period of time the biggest left-wing party in terms of membership. In 1993, when the Communist Party was re-established, the SPT lost most of its members. Failing to present a political face of its own, lacking strong leadership and suffering from internal bureaucratic struggles, the SPT underwent a steady decline becoming completely marginal. Radical communist parties also declined after 1993.[76]

The Communist Party of Russian Federation (CPRF) remained the only visible opposition to the corrupt and authoritarian Yeltsin regime for the whole period of 1993–98. And it was also the kind of opposition the regime allowed and even sometimes welcomed. Under the leadership of Gennady Ziuganov the party combined nostalgia for the Soviet past with acceptance of free market economic policies and nationalist, sometimes anti-semitic rhetoric. The ideological 'innovation' of the Ziuganov leadership was the replacement of old Soviet Marxism-Leninism by the concept of Eurasianism or neo-Slavophilism. As Vladimir Belenkin writes in *Monthly Review*:

> Like Russian Westernism, the Eurasian ideology is a primarily essentialist, hyper-rhetorical and performative discourse. Whereas neo-liberal ideological production seeks to break up the controlling codes of social behaviour and the cultural patterns of the Soviet period, and to set free the acquisitive impulse of capitalist desire and consumerism, the Eurasian project is an attempt to exploit what is left of the symbolic energies of the past in the interests of national capital. What they share is a view of the masses as an inert object of ideological indoctrination and manipulation.[77]

The policies of the CPRF leadership generated a lot of discontent among both activists and voters. In 1993 younger communist activists resurrected the Youth Communist League (the *Komsomol*). The new Komsomol emerged as a formation with a rather eclectic ideology uniting young people with very different views – from left-wing social democrats to communist traditionalists. While 'the old comrades' were constantly moving from socialist positions to nationalist ones, the Komsomol became the pole of attraction not only for young communist activists but also for many independent leftists of all ages. As a result the Komsomol absorbed some of the original ideology of the Party of Labour as well as some of the organizing culture of the radical communist parties of the early 1990s.

In 1999, when the leaders of Russian Komsomol broke decisively with the CPRF, their organization split. The situation was made worse by the failure of the Komsomol leadership to organize a real strategic debate within their organization and present a clear perspective to the membership. RKSM retained most members and branches. However, in order to survive, its leadership decided to make an opportunistic deal with the Stalinist far left and form an electoral block with them.

At the same time, the independent left was re-emerging in different parts of Russia. In 1999 a populist leftist candidate, Alexander Burkov, finished second in the governor's race in Sverdlov province, the captital of which is Ekaterinburg, the third largest city in Russia and a former stronghold of Yeltsin. In Moscow, radical groups such as the Left Vanguard and Independent Socialist University made their presence felt.

For those trying to relaunch the socialist project in Russia the German PDS clearly served as a model. But this new left remained weak, lacking both political experience and involvement in popular struggles.

The failures of the socialist left in Eastern Europe can be explained by wrong policies, lack of experience, absence of a political tradition and cultural contradictions. After the collapse of the communist regimes both the language of socialism and the traditional values of the labour movement were discredited, though not as much as liberal journalists and ideologues expected. However, there were also objective factors that worked against anti-capitalist forces. During the ten years that followed the events of 1989 most of the economies of the region declined. That brought about not only tremendous sufferings for the majority of the people but also marginalization and demoralization of the workers. Mass movements often radicalize in the period of crisis but building a new organization during such periods is incredibly difficult, if not impossible. The weakness of the mass resistance frustrated radical activists, many of whom dropped out of the struggle. In these circumstances the left groups were either becoming sectarian or turning into intellectual clubs, sometimes involved in electoral politics.

Another source of weakness of the left is the weakness of capitalist development itself. The structure of capitalism in the East is not complete and the awareness of the new contradictions in society is often lacking. But it is this weakness of the capitalist development that in the long run makes the appearance of the radical left necessary. The system created by the International Monetary Fund and local elites has no chance of resolving the problems of these societies because it is itself the main cause of these problems. There is simply no prospect of a successful bourgeois evolution. And that means that the left with its own alternatives is objectively needed.

The Pluralist Left

The modern left movement cannot and must not be homogeneous, since the working masses are not uniform. In this sense the situation has changed radically since the early years of the twentieth century, when trade unions and socialist parties were being established in Europe. Differences of qualifications, incomes and culture within the working class existed then as well, but in the period since, they have increased dramatically.

The social base of left parties is now no longer made up only of industrial workers. At one pole is a mass of unqualified workers and of people active in the 'informal sector', while at the other are operators of computerized equipment and highly qualified workers in traditional industry. White-collar and blue-collar workers find that they have a multitude of common interests, but a quite different psychology. Scientific workers recognize themselves as a 'new proletariat', but are in no hurry to join organizations of the 'old' labour movement. Representatives of various races, religions and cultures are not only united by common work and shared problems, but are also divided by traditions and prejudices. This motley world of labour cannot be united and organized mechanically. This does not mean that unity and a united organization are impossible in principle. It is the diversity of the working masses that makes the task of political unification especially important. The only organization that can be effective in such circumstances is one that is democratic and pluralist, combining features of both a party and a movement and, to some degree, even of a coalition. As theoreticians of the German PDS note, social mobilization under present-day conditions is impossible unless old concepts of discipline are decisively rejected. 'New, open organizational forms' are essential.[78] This openness, together perhaps with a certain organizational looseness, is at the same time a guarantee against opportunism, since the leadership can no longer be sure of the unconditional support and loyalty of the membership base.

Trotskyist critics of Stalinism, while accepting the idea of a disciplined vanguard party, constantly discovered in it a 'problem of leadership'. In reality this was the problem of the centralized structure and 'factory discipline' of the old workers' movement. The late twentieth century is seeing the opportunity open up for the triumph of a new approach. It is no doubt for this reason that the Brazilian Workers' Party and the German PDS, despite their obvious looseness and the contradictions of their politics, have been the two most effective left parties of the 'new generation'.

At the beginning of the century the 'model' for leftists was the German social democracy. After 1917 the same role was claimed by the Bolsheviks, and then by the Maoist Communist Party of China and insurgent organizations founded in line with the initiatives of Ernesto 'Che' Guevara. Now there is no such model, and nor can there be. The German PDS, the Brazilian Workers' Party and the Mexican Zapatistas are phenomena of the same order precisely because they are unlike one another. The 'new wave' left movement cannot be homogeneous; it is united precisely by the fact that in dealing with common tasks and goals it does not employ a standard form or single model. On the whole, the organizational forms are changeable and unstable, since they are determined on the basis of extremely contradictory practice.

However great the value of pluralism, it is essential to have unifying and consolidating mechanisms that make it possible to take common decisions, and, most importantly, to carry them out. Without a common organization various groups of workers will not only be unable to defend their common interests (not to speak of changing society), but will be unable to solve their specific, 'private' problems. The lack of solidarity and help from 'other quarters' will invariably result in defeat.

Heterogeneity is a characteristic of 'new wave' left organizations irrespective of where they carry on their activity – in Europe, in Asia or in Latin America. In New Zealand, where a sharp turn to the right by the old Labour Party forced socialists to create the NewLabour [sic – one word] Party as an alternative to it, the influence of the new party at first remained confined to traditional sections of old Labour's working class base. This situation ended when New Labour joined with other organizations representing the indigenous Maori population (*Mana*

Motuhake) and the women's and environmental movements to form the Alliance. Originally the Alliance did not look very stable. As one of the observers noted: 'critiques of market-driven "development" provide a necessary but not sufficient condition for a coherent Alliance alternative. Any broad eco-left program confronts long-standing divisions of interest.' One the one hand there was a contradiction between the push for growth-led Keynesian policies of the traditional socialists and green ideals of a steady-state economy. One the other hand there were cultural differences.

> Ideological tensions are also evident between political generations. Within NewLabour, for example, older members seek to restore trade union solidarity and the egalitarian principles of threatened public institutions such as health, education, and housing. Younger activists (along with Green and Mana Motuhake members) have been shaped by the identity-centered policies of feminism, ecology, and anti-racism.[79]

However the Alliance survived and even grew stronger throughout the 1990s. The contradictions did not disappear but democratic political practice and mutual tolerance allowed all these movements to stay together. A non-dogmatic though sometimes eclectic political culture was developing. As one of the Alliance documents stated: 'Sometimes a close approach to the ideal is better than perfection itself.'[80]

Turkey provides another example of the way in which the unification of various forces has allowed the forming of a 'new wave' left party. Here the Party of Freedom and Solidarity emerged onto the political scene in the late 1990s. A first step toward the unification of the left was the founding by ten revolutionary groups in 1995 of the Unified Socialist Party (BSP). It was only after this that the formation of a broader organization – the Party of Freedom and Solidarity – became possible. Turkish leftists identified themselves as a coalition of 'democratic modernizers of Marxist and non-Marxist inspiration'. They promised to be engaged in 'all struggles against all sorts of injustice and oppression without sacrificing any of them for the sake of others'.[81]

The Party of Freedom and Solidarity is described by its leader Ufak Uras as 'pluralist' and 'transparent', a distinctive coalition 'of the revolutionary left, of socialists, of rank and file social democrats, of feminists, of greens, of anti-militarists, of anarchists, etc.'. In the words of Uras, the task of the party, which in the course of several months in 1996 and 1997 grew to have 30,000 members, consists of 'refounding the left'. In a certain sense, this party is throwing down a challenge to all of Turkey's traditional political culture with its authoritarianism and clientelism.

> Our experience represents a break with arbitrary behaviour by leaders, with hierarchical models, with submissiveness to orders from above, with the professionalization of politics, with the taking of decisions at levels remote from their execution, and with the passive consumption of politics.[82]

The party's founders have managed to overcome the tradition of sectarianism and extremism that characterized the Turkish left in the 1970s, and which continued to make itself felt throughout the 1980s. At the same time as the left-centrist parties that lay claim to the role of the local social democracy have moved further and further to the right, transforming themselves into faceless groups serving opportunist leaders, the left has been able to unite in a single organization, issuing a challenge both to the neo-liberalism that holds sway in the country, and to political Islam. The process of unifying the various socialist and revolutionary groups took several years and, significantly, occurred against the background of a spontaneous rise of the workers' movement.

The collaboration of neo-liberals and Islamicists in the Turkish government following the 1996 elections – something which seems paradoxical at first glance – led to a situation in which the left was the only ideological and political alternative. In the conditions of Turkey, the Party of Freedom and Solidarity is not only the bearer of socialist ideas but also the most consistent of the defenders of civil liberties and secular principles. In the view of party activists, this is both the organization's strength and its weakness, since much of its activity is devoted to defending general democratic rights. To a significant degree the same could be said of the People's Democratic Party in Indonesia. This party grew quickly in the late 1990s as the wave of mass protest against the Suharto dictatorship swelled. The country's rapid industrialization created the conditions for the growth of the labour movement, which took on mass dimensions at the same time as the need for democracy was ripening in society.

In the Philippines the left also made an important step towards unity. After many years of sectarian confrontations it was not easy. In 1999 the founding congress of the Socialist Party of Labour (SPP) braught together representatives from various traditions in the Philippine left: those who left the formerly Moscow-aligned Philippine Communist Party (PKP), the pro-Maoist Communist Party of the Philippines (CPP), and the left wing of the Philippine Democratic Socialist Party. Socialists from the two main national liberation movements in the country also attended, including delegates from the Cordillera Peoples' Liberation Army (CPLA) and from movements struggling for self-determination for the Moro people.

The late 1990s produced another important political phenomenon which may have important long-term consequences: the far left entered parliamentary politics. While social democrats all over the world, as well as some parties to the left of social democracy, were moving to the right, frustrated votes turned to the radical groups which earlier were considered to be marginal. At the same time some groups of the far left managed to overcome their own sectarian traditions and rivalries and created coalitions that became a real electoral force. From the point of view of the past these coalitions could look odd – often bringing together former Maoists, Trotskyists and traditionalist communists. But they are also a very modern phenomenon, representing the necessity of combining different radical traditions inside the new pluralist left. In Denmark and Norway, where left socialist parties gradually moved towards social democracy, these coalitions of the far left filled the emerging political vacuum.[83] They managed to get elected to the national parliaments. The Trotskyist Scottish Socialist Party managed to get one deputy in the Assembly of Scotland. In the Netherlands, the ex-Maoist Socialist Party (dubbed the Tomato Party) increased its influence. The progress of this party was impressive indeed. In 1974 it had five municipal deputies, in 1999 it had 223. Its parliamentary representation in 1998 increased from two to five seats. Between

1994 and 1998 9,000 people joined the party putting the number of its members up to 25,000. In 1999 it became the fifth biggest party of the country and won its first Euro MP's seat. But the biggest political sensation was the success of French Trotskyists in the European elections of 1999.

The joint list formed by *Lutte Ouvrier* (LO) and *League Communiste Revolutionnaire* (LCR), the two most important Trotskyist formations in France, won 5.2 per cent or almost 1 million votes. The leaders of the coalition, Arlette Laguiller and Alain Krivine, became European deputies. Most important, the LO-LCR list achieved impressive results in the regions that were the power base of the traditional left, sometimes capturing 7 or even 9 per cent of the vote.

'Five revolutionary deputies – one man and four women – will now sit in the European parliament, working with other revolutionary deputies to form a strong parliamentary group', reported *Green Left Weekly* enthusiastically.[84] And the paper of LCR stated that 'the far left has affirmed itself as a significant, stable political force'.[85] However, in reality the LO-LCR list achieved its success not so much as a result of its own strength but more as a result of the crisis of the traditional mainstream left. Most of all, it was a punishment for the old Communist Party, which participated in the coalition government. It is also very telling that the 1999 election, which for the first time in history put a Trotskyist group in the European parliament was the biggest defeat ever suffered by social democrats: for the first time since 1979, when the parliament began to be directly elected, they lost their majority there. The biggest losses were suffered by the New Labour in Britain and the German Social Democrats. 'The results devastated Labour's representation in Europe and were a big factor in ending the Socialist Group's dominance in the European parliament', commented a left Labour paper.[86]

The French Communist Party, which was in government together with the Socialists, also lost votes while retaining the same number of deputies, and the Spanish *Izquierda Unida* (United Left) lost five MEPs. Even Rifondazione lost one deputy, though it was not such a bad result given the split it suffered few months before the election. At the same time, the parties that had proved their radicalism, mostly through a strong campaign against NATO and the bombing of Serbia, all did quite well. In

Greece the three left parties that opposed the bombings represented a combined 20 per cent of the vote: the Greek Communist Party, the left coalition *Synaspismos* and *Dikki*, a left social democratic party, won 8.5 per cent, 5 per cent and 6.9 per cent of the vote respectively.

At a time when the mainstream lacks principles, radicalism is rewarding. And that creates new opportunities for those who dare to express their opposition to the system.

Finally, the left wing of Social Democracy is still alive, though not well. Both the New Labour project in England and Schroeder's *'Neue Mitte'* (New Centre) strategy in Germany encounter growing resistance within their own parties. The social democratic left still hopes to win back the old parties to their initial socialist cause. This approach has failed so far, and most probably will continue to fail in the future. However, there are progressive currents within these parties and they will have a role to play in the debate shaping the new project of the left.[87]

The eclecticism of today's pluralist left is not a virtue. However, it represents a necessary stage of development of the movement and is a great step forward after the years of bureaucratic ideological discipline of the old social democratic and communist movements. Eclecticism is a necessary evil for the left in overcoming its own sectarian traditions. And a new, more organic ideology will be formed in the process of struggle. What is essential however, is that the struggle continues. The left that tries to accommodate itself to capitalism has no future and no chance to put forward any new ideas.

Between Resistance and 'Constructive Work'

Municipal politics is becoming the main strategic area of work for the 'new wave' left. For the social democratic and communist movements of the past, municipal socialism was only a stage along the road to winning power at the centre, but for the new generation of left parties it is becoming a laboratory of change. In theory, municipal socialism makes it possible to combine an orientation to state property with decentralization, with transforming the structures of power, and with using market stimuli.

In practice, everything is far more complex. Municipal socialism has to create and reproduce its own local power base, confronting numerous problems along the way.

The Party of Democratic Socialism in Germany encountered serious problems when its representatives, who were fiercely rejected by the political establishment, came to head municipalities. The policies of PDS administrators often frustrated the supporters of the party. In the 1999 European elections Democratic Socialists gained votes in every German *Länd* with the exception of Meklenburg-Vorpommern where they were in power together with Social Democrats. At the same time the PDS had its own 'success stroies' as well – and that was reflected by the growing proportion of votes the party won in the communal elections in other parts of East Germany, including conservative Saxony.

The fact that East Germany was swallowed by the west meant that the 'new *Länder*' did not have their own large bourgeoisie. The small and middle bourgeois in the east felt themselves to be restricted and denied their rights. At a result, the party in these regions received support not only from workers, but also from many small and middle entrepreneurs. The socialist municipal councillors who were elected in the eastern *Länder* faced a difficult dilemma: were they only representatives of the workers, or did they represent the 'common interests of the district'?[88]

When the situation in each case calls for resistance to the Western authorities and large Western corporations, these contradictions might be relegated to a secondary level, but the party's activists and theoreticians cannot fail to be conscious of them. Otto Theel, elected to the local council of the small city of Neuruppin on the PDS list, admitted in the party's journal that he was troubled by 'internal conflict'.[89] In essence, this is a problem shared by any left-wing local administration in capitalist society. There cannot be any ready-made answer and, by definition, any success in solving the problem can only be partial. The only way to overcome these contradictions is to keep moving forward, and to maintain a democratic dialogue between the administrators, the party activists and the mass movements. This dialogue is by no means always pleasant for the administrators, but in the final analysis it guarantees the party's vitality.

In the late 1980s and during the 1990s Latin American leftists scored successes in such large business and industrial centres as San Salvador, Caracas, Montevideo, São Paulo and Mexico City. In many cases their practical work in the municipalities was highly successful. Experience has shown that successes in large cities does not guarantee that the left will come to power on the national level, but they are an important stage in the struggle to transform society.

Evaluating the work of the municipalities administered by the PT in Brazil, Lula came to the conclusion that thanks to this experience the party had become more 'mature', while not becoming less radical: 'a party begins to mature not when it becomes moderate, but when it gains consciousness of its responsibilities'.[90] In practice, however, by no means all of the PT's municipal policies have had the desired result, and quite serious conflicts have arisen between the more moderate administrators and the more radical activists. It was such conflicts that led ultimately to the defeat of the administration of Luisa Erundina in São Paulo. The paradox was that the electors who voted for a left-wing city administration hoped that it would be at once both radical and competent, ensuring concrete changes for the better. In 1997, when the former insurgents in El Salvador won majorities in the municipalities of the capital and of six large cities, activists of the movement noted that people expected them to perform, while the vote was at the same time for 'radical change'.[91] Success at the local level can be gained through an innovative approach and through radical decisions that change the rules of the game. But at the same time a left-wing local administration, however radical it might be, cannot simply ignore the logic of the capitalist system. From the very beginning, therefore, it finds itself in an ambiguous situation, subject to pressure from opposite sides. Without constant pressure from below, a left administration simply has no prospects; it will be crushed by the force of the system. Criticism and support are mutually interlinked. The task of left-wing municipal authorities consists of being open to such pressure from below, as a liberal administration is not.

When describing his years as head of the Greater London Council, Ken Livingstone stressed that he took many of his most successful decisions under pressure 'from below'. In the municipalities administered by the Brazilian Workers' Party as well, the principle of open decision-making was a guarantee of popularity. The revenge taken by the Tory government on the GLC was a consequence of the council's success; the government's supporters had no chance of winning an open electoral struggle in the London municipality. The government was therefore obliged to take a step without precedent in conditions of democracy, abolishing city self-government in the British capital. Livingstone notes:

> Leftwingers in parliament are ten times more effective when there's community or industrial action outside. And community and industrial action are much more effective when there is a group of MPs supporting their struggle on the floor of the House of Commons.[92]

But if 'parliamentary socialism' can exist for a considerable period in isolation from the mass movement, municipal socialism cannot survive without its support. This has been shown by the fate of many left administrations.

In the 1990s, the question of the relationship between responsibility and principled opposition is posed sharply every time the left breaks out of its political ghetto and confronts the problems of rule. Fortunately, the enemies of the left movement often prompt it to make the correct decisions.

If Cardoso's social policy had been a little more flexible, the disagreements within the PT would have been even stronger. In just the same way, the German PDS in its dealings with the social democrats was torn, to use the words of one of its critics, 'between coalition and opposition'.[93] Fortunately for the left, the self-satisfied obstinacy and primitive anti-communism that are typical of Western 'Greens' and social democrats made a union with them impossible, and saved the PDS as an opposition party.

Where the situation is not so clear, the left is doomed to balance constantly on the edge of internal crisis. Strikingly similar situations have arisen in such dissimilar countries as the US, Russia and India. The heterogeneity of the left movement transforms the slogan 'unity of the left forces' into an unremitting task that has to be done over and over again, while at the same time optimal policies must be chosen for dealing with the question of power and responsibility. The problem is not only one of tactical differences, but also of different political cultures. Every group has its own policy of alliances, which may ultimately work against the consolidation of the left forces. Even within a single party, sharp disagreements are likely to arise on the question of partners. Coalitions are naturally tempting, since a serious party cannot simply say 'no' to society; it has to engage in real work here and now on behalf of its social base, and this means that in certain cases it cannot avoid 'constructive collaboration' with the establishment. The question of the basis for this collaboration, and the goals, is something else entirely. In India, despite almost twenty years of discussion on the unity of the left, the real results up until the mid-1990s were not great. The reasons were not only to be found in sectarianism, dogmatism and the ambitions of leaders. 'Left unity cannot be held hostage to the compulsions of alliances with bourgeois parties',[94] declared Naghushan Patnaik, Chairman of the CPI-ML (Liberation), when greeting a congress of the 'official' Communist Party. However, such an approach requires a serious review of tactics and strategy on the part of each of the organizations that are striving for unification.

The choice between 'oppositionism' and 'constructiveness' will always be a matter of blundering about in the dark so long as the left lacks clear criteria of success. These in turn cannot exist while the goals of the left remain obscure. The heterogeneity of the left movement does not remove the need for a unifying ideology. Indeed, the differences between the forces that make up the support base of the left mean that such an ideology is a vital necessity. One of the participants in the PDS's discussion programme, Dr Joachim Hempel, made this point as follows:

> Without socialist motives, practical interests and a corresponding new consciousness, a democratic majority will simply not come about, while an intolerable social situation, antisocial relationships and the destruction of the social welfare system [*Sozialabbau*] will not on their own lead to spontaneous resistance.[95]

Success for the left depends on its capacity to be firm in its resistance to capitalism. But the pressure to be 'constructive' (working within the system) also grows, together with the success. In late 1990s, parties and forces that place themselves to the left of Social Democracy in many countries achieved such a degree of success that in many cases societies became ungovernable without them. That was the case of the PDS in some parts of East Germany. The Left Party in Sweden gained 12 per cent in the 1998 elections and the Social Democrats were not able to rule without its consent. In Italy the government of post-communist

Social Democrats was not able to survive without votes provided by the deputies from Rifondazione. This caused the split in the party. A few months earlier parties of the left won parliamentary elections in the Ukraine. Communists took 27 per cent of the vote, Socialists and Agrarians 9.4 per cent and even the far left Progressive Socialist Party managed to enter parliament with 4.4 per cent. While the liberal press was full of noise about 'the threat to reforms', analysts agreed that the population was radicalizing: 'Voting for the Communists was a protest, and it's a positive one because people did not go out in the street with axes; they manifested it legally.'[96] In Russia the left was also growing. In autumn 1998 the new government was formed by Evgeny Primakov. It included Communist ministers and depended on the leftist majority in parliament. After eight months of Primakov's experiment, the country was saved from the financial and economic catastrophe which the new government had inherited in August 1998. However, the very success of Primakov led him to political failure. The ruling elites of Russia recovered from the August disaster and started a counter-offensive. In May 1999 Primakov was forced to resign.

The lesson we have to learn from the Primakov experiment is not that unique. Reformers who try to cure the illness of the system are usually devoured by the system as soon as they fulfil their task. But at the same time reforms really can make a difference. The people expect the left in office to be radically different from the liberals. But the left does not have enough strength to change the system. Is it possible for the left to be involved in the daily management of the system without losing its identity as the force of resistance and change? Maybe it is not, but that is exactly what the people want it to do.

Social democrats, at their best, were able to manage capitalist institutions in such a way that it really made difference. Since then, everything has changed. The 'New Realism' praised by Tony Blair, Massimo D'Alema and other social democratic leaders in the 1990s is exactly about not being different from the neo-liberal right. In the late 1990s the left must learn to be different again. But in the long run success will depend not on management technologies but on democracy, on the ability of the left to express the needs of the people and the ability of the people to control their leftist representatives.

Implementing the principle of class politics poses a serious challenge, especially in a period when the social structure itself is undergoing profound changes. A class approach cannot replace a policy of broad alliances; society is not only divided into 'two classes', as the popularizers of Bolshevism thought. But 'class' unification is a first step, an initial condition without which the success of a 'broad' alliance is inconceivable. The politics of the left, formulating common demands, ideas and outlooks for various social layers, helps in transforming the atomized masses and corporate social groups into a class, conscious of its role and mission in society.

From Networking to Challenging the System

The twenty-first century has not yet begun, but sociologists have already characterized it as a time of 'network structures'.[97] This is quite correct; 'vertical' models of organization and rule are more and more often failing to yield results. But it does not by any means follow that the need for parties and trade unions is disappearing. They simply need to undergo changes. From being hierarchical organizations aiming at a 'monolithic' character, they need to transform themselves into flexible structures, linking and coordinating different struggles and actions. The key task of a party is to ensure hegemony. A party brings elements of consciousness to a movement, it brings purposefulness and coordination, and transforms casual, spontaneous actions into a united offensive.

The globalization of economic life does not mean the end of political parties, but simply broadens their tasks. The slogan 'Act locally, think globally' is correct only in so far as local struggles are coordinated on the regional, national and global levels. Without this, no 'global' thinking will help. The coordinating of actions is becoming the main task of political organizations. The link between acting and thinking does not come about of itself; it is a political task, which needs to be carried out if parties and organizations are to be established. The 'new wave' left is constantly encountering this problem, irrespective of where the events are unfolding – on the streets of Paris, in the jungles of Chiapas or in German municipalities. The newspaper *Neues Deutschland*, which is close to the PDS, wrote that the Zapatista uprising served as an example of how it was possible to connect 'local resistance with global development'.[98] The PDS itself is a party that is trying, if not always successfully, to link protest that arises in the west with resistance in the east, parliamentary work in the capital with municipal work in the 'backyard' of the united Germany.

In the mid-1990s the various forms of organized solidarity on the inter-party and international level remained in an embryonic state. Alongside the 'Socialist International', which was increasingly becoming a vague alliance of populist, moderate liberal, social democratic and radical parties, the São Paulo Forum, established by Latin American leftists, emerged as a serious coordinating structure. The pluralism of the São Paulo Forum, which encompassed communists, left social democrats, radical reformists and revolutionaries, reflected the natural heterogeneity of the continent's left forces. But while demonstrating the ability of the left to unify itself, the forum did not become a genuine coordinating structure.

The collaboration of left parties in Europe has not even reached the Latin American level, despite periodic meetings between leaders and fine slogans about a struggle 'for a new Europe, for a Europe of a new civilization of labour'.[99] Not even the existence of the European parliament, around which joint work could in theory be organized, has been of any help.

The heart of the problem evidently lies in the fact that the epoch of globalization requires far more concentrated and intensive collaboration on the level of concrete actions, while at the same time the new cultural heterogeneity of the left and its natural aversion to the centralized bureaucracy of the past are preventing the creation of unified leadership structures.

The world has changed, and the old forms of the left movement are turning out to be unsuited to solving the new problems. Organizations are trying to survive by demonstrating their loyalty to the ruling elites, but the more inoffensive they become, the less interesting anyone finds them. The time has come for a change of organizational forms.

Gramsci wrote:

At a certain stage along their historical path social groups break with their traditional parties. This means a break both with the traditional parties and with their particular forms of organization. The people who make up and represent these parties and lead them are no longer seen as real spokespeople for the class or section of the class. When such crises arise, the situation becomes very difficult, even dangerous, since the possibility arises of solving these crises with the help of violence, and the possibility is present of action by sinister forces represented by providential individuals.[100]

To change the world the left has to change itself. In fact, as the Argentinian historian Horatio Tarcus wrote, sectarian forms of leftism were adequate to the situation of defensive ideological struggles of the 1980s. But to regain the initiative the left has to find a way to be ideological without being sectarian. The political left can grow only in parallel with the social left: an authentic revolutionary organization doesn't grow just through increasing its membership, but only when it roots itself in social movements as well.[101] If the left does not meet the challenge of the times, other forces will become the mouthpieces of protest. Socialists must again issue a challenge to the established order. Otherwise, political barbarians will do this for them.

Conclusion: The Stage We are In

The twentieth century began as an epoch of enthusiastic faith in progress, but as it draws to a close, the attitude toward progress is one of profound disappointment. Faith in progress and disappointment with it are both subjective matters. There is no question, however, that the twentieth century has done more than any other to reveal the limited and contradictory nature of social progress, just as it has shown the obvious dangers associated with technical progress. Even when the century began, none of this was really new; it is enough to recall how Marx in his writings on British rule in India observed that the cost of progress was appallingly high.

Nevertheless, the numerous critiques of progress that have been produced by leftists (or former leftists) have failed to answer the key logical question, which at the same time is very simple: is there progress in history? Yes or no? If not, then how does one explain everything that has happened so far? How did we manage to crawl out of the caves? How did we make the transition from feudalism to capitalism, from absolutism to democracy? If there was indeed progress in the past, where has it got to now? Why is there such confidence that the past has gone for good, and that the present order is unshakeable? And even if we believe that progress has stopped, has slipped into the past, has become obsolete, then what happens from now on? Is it really logical to suppose that the future will mechanically repeat the present? Even Fukuyama, in proclaiming the end of history, did not venture to assert that history would never resume.

The intellectual capitulation of the left in the period since 1989–91 has been based on an undeclared but very profound inner conviction that history has come to an end once and for all. We have no need to fear the judgement of our descendants, since they will not be any different from us. We do not have to answer to anyone or for anything, since we are not linked to them in any way. Responsibility is inconceivable to people who are unaware of connections of time. Hamlet lamented that the

149

times were out of joint; leftists, unlike Hamlet, are not trying to thrust the times back into their socket.

Is this really true of all leftists? Not strictly, and as soon as someone starts to act, all the criminality, cowardice and impotence of those who cloak their inactivity with arguments about new times and natural limitations is laid bare.

Reaction is a natural part of development. What has suffered a collapse has not been social progress, but our simplistic understanding of it – together with the policies of those who hoped that, by climbing on board social progress, they could profit from the linear advance of history.

An epoch of reaction does not demand heroism. It requires firmness and sobriety, and an ability to swim against the current. Reaction always seems more powerful than it is in reality. A new potential for social protest has to ripen in society, and new demands have to be formulated. It may be necessary to wait for many years before this happens. But it is well known how wrong Lenin was when he predicted, a few months before the February revolution, that a revolution in Russia was something that his generation would not live to see.

The need in the late twentieth century is for a re-evaluation of all preceding development. But this will be impossible if we rest solely on the experience of the last two decades, as fashionable Western intellectuals are accustomed to do.

In the mid-1950s Soviet historians encountered a methodological problem: how should they characterize the epoch from the fifteenth to the seventeenth centuries? On the one hand, this period saw great geographical discoveries, the Reformation, the peasant wars in Germany, the implanting of bourgeois property relations, and the revolutions in Holland and Britain. On the other hand, it witnessed continuing feudal wars; the imposing of the 'second serfdom' on the peasantry of Germany and Eastern Europe; the inquisition; and the Counter-Reformation. Some scholars saw here the death-agony of the Middle Ages, an epoch of late feudalism. Others wrote of an 'epoch of early bourgeois revolutions'. It was not only the Reformation and the struggles of the Dutch for liberation from feudal Spain that were laying the basis for the new society. To a striking degree, the dynamics and archetypes of later revolutions were already to be observed in fifteenth-century Bohemia, in the Hussite wars. Everything was present there, from a triumphant popular uprising to the establishing of an oligarchy, from defence of the homeland to expansionism. The victorious movement, after vanquishing all its external enemies, unexpectedly fell victim to its internal weaknesses, and itself opened the way for restoration.

The Utraquisten and Taboriten of the Hussite Wars became the prototypes for the two revolutionary parties that are encountered repeatedly in modern history – the Presbyterians and Independents in Britain, the Girondins and Jacobins in France, and the Mensheviks and Bolsheviks in Russia. The failures suffered by the first revolutions were repeated in the successes of those that followed; times of radical change alternated with periods of a reaction that was no less radical and, in its own way, dynamic. The historical cycle that began somewhere in the mid-fifteenth century with the campaigns of the Hussites and with important geographical discoveries culminated in the struggle of the parliament against the king in seventeenth-century Britain. The first 'classical' revolution, this already spelt the end of feudalism. Victorious and at the same time incomplete, it provided the generations that followed with new ideas and new models for imitation. Concepts of what was possible and permissible changed radically. But history, as it were, then paused. The cycle had been completed.

In essence, the historians who wrote about late feudalism and those who spoke of a period of early bourgeois revolutions were equally correct. The epoch of transition was both one and the other.

The collapse of the Soviet Union has forced the Russian left to turn once again to making a study of history – to discussing the past, this time applying the lessons of the past to the future. Aleksandr Buzgalin has argued that the transition to socialism is not a discrete revolutionary act, but constitutes a whole epoch, a 'non-linear, contradictory, international process'.[1]

This is in line with Lenin's thinking: 'A social revolution is not a single battle, but an epoch that encompasses a whole series of battles around all sorts of economic and democratic changes that can end only in the expropriation of the bourgeoisie.'[2] During the First World War the Bolshevik leader expected that the proletariat would have to endure 'perhaps another half-century of enslavement'.[3] Nevertheless, Lenin could not have imagined quite how difficult, painful and drawn-out this process would be. The victory of the October revolution inclined him to a more optimistic view, but at the end of his life he was again beset with doubts. The Russian Revolution of 1917 should in fact be regarded as one among a series of initial, unsuccessful attempts at the socialist transformation of society. Other ill-fated essays in revolution are destined to follow. Buzgalin writes:

> An effort needs to be made to understand the outcome of these first attempts at a practical breakthrough to socialism. In some ways this experience can be compared with the attempts that were made in the fifteenth and sixteenth centuries to carry through the transition from feudalism to bourgeois society, for example in renaissance Italy. In each case genuine elements of the new society appeared. But these elements arose out of blood . . . amid the smoke of battle . . . and met with a tragic end. They were followed either by the restoration of the feudal order and the Austrian yoke, or by a dependent type of *nomen-klatura* capitalism. . . . The tragedy of the Renaissance, however, was succeeded by the revolutionary struggle of Garibaldi, and the ideal of the human individual free of feudal constraints triumphed throughout the world. I am convinced that the tragedy of twentieth-century socialism will ultimately be no less optimistic, but only if we succeed in drawing the lessons from this defeat.[4]

By contrast, the political scientist Aleksandr Tarasov argues that the processes in Russia, China and the other countries of 'real socialism' were really only late bourgeois revolutions that met with failure to the degree that they sought to proceed beyond the bounds of their legitimate historical tasks. Their orientation toward socialism linked them, however, with the beginning of a 'new revolutionary cycle'.[5]

It is obvious that these two points of view do not necessarily exclude one another. The 'late bourgeois' revolutions were at the same time 'early socialist'. This historical cycle began with the Paris Commune and, after failing to realize its possibilities there, found its expression in the great revolutions of the twentieth century, the Russian and the Chinese. It culminated in the 1950s and 1960s with the people's wars in Cuba and Vietnam. The final surge of the revolutionary wave saw the coming to office of the Popular Unity in Chile, and the events of 1974 and 1975 in Portugal.

It was no accident that the anti-capitalist revolutions of the twentieth century took place in countries where a fully realized bourgeois society had not come into being. Not merely Russia and China, but also such countries as Chile and Portugal were on the periphery of the capitalist world system. This meant not only that they were dependent on the 'centre', but also that the formation of bourgeois social relations within them was incomplete. The fact that capitalism in general has not been fated to achieve the absolute perfection and 'purity' of which its ideologues dream is something else again.

At first national-democratic or national-liberation in character, the revolutionary movements swiftly and inevitably broke out of the framework of 'bourgeois social change', but were incapable of creating socialism. Their tragedy was preordained. They carried through the work of capitalism, but could not do this without placing capitalism itself in question. In exactly the same way Western European reformism, even in its moderate forms, exceeded the limits of the bourgeois order, although in essence it was trying merely to improve and modernize capitalism. The tragedy of reformism was exactly the same as the tragedy of the revolutions. It could not achieve its goals without destroying the society it was trying to preserve.

While moving outside the bounds of capitalism, the revolutions in the developing countries could not avoid creating their own mongrel forms of the new society. Democratic tasks were ultimately carried out, though only at the cost of liquidating the post-revolutionary regimes. However, the democracies that arose on this basis were at best pale copies of the Western originals, and at times direct parodies of them. Late capitalism made democracy its slogan, but not its practice. In precisely the same way, the triumph of a single world system has made capitalism universal, but far from all-pervasive. Through the incompleteness of bourgeois modernization, and the impossibility of completing it, the preconditions for new revolutionary crises are being created.

The epoch of the early socialist movements has come to an end. What happens now? Will the pause last for long? And how will it end? To a significant degree this depends on leftists themselves, and on their ability to understand the lessons of history.

Perry Anderson in his book *A Zone of Engagement* argues that neo-liberalism will remain the dominant ideology until socialists are able to offer 'feasible alternatives'.[6] The problem, though, does not lie in any lack of feasible theories, but in the weakness of the political organizations that espouse them. Concepts of democratic planning, of a renovated mixed economy, and of market and post-market socialism are discussed in the most detailed manner in academic circles, and no one has yet proved that in their 'pure' form these are less serious constructs than the ideas of the neo-liberals.[7] Ultimately, as the critic of Marxist orthodoxy Alec Nove correctly observes, 'the Marxist vision is not more utopian than "perfect competition"'.[8] In reality, however, the virtues and shortcomings of theory can be determined only by practice. The ideas and opinions of Lenin or Trotsky would hardly have aroused such interest throughout the world if on 7 November 1917 the Petrograd workers had not managed to storm the Winter Palace.

The failures of the Soviet system made socialists suspicious about any kind of central planning. At the same time they became more and more enthusiastic about the market. The Green parties were leading the way, formulating their own view of a democratic economy, 'combining public services with a plethora of modestly sized cooperatives and partnerships, financed by banks with selective investment criteria'.[9] Theorists of market socialism followed the same path, rejecting 'the fetishism of public ownership'.[10] While they did not embrace private property either, the emphasis was put on different models of stakeholding economy, allowing everyone access to property rights, and on community ownership.

> The duality of private and public ownership stems from the historical realities of the agricultural and industrial ages, reflecting the deprivation and denial of potential of those times. Community ownership strategies offer one key to fair and just economy, in keeping with the post-industrial need for everyone to achieve complete personal fulfilment and development.[11]

Communal property looks much more attractive than giant capitalist corporations and Soviet-style monster ministries. Unfortunately, the modern economy needs coordination above and beyond the level of community. Looking for answers, many socialist theorists insist on combining capitalist efficiency with public property and democracy.

Robin Blackburn writes:

> The new models of 'market socialism' share with the similar, though not identical, concept of the 'socialized market' a notion of economic institutions which is not monist. On the one hand, this means that no single economic institution is expected to guarantee all socially desirable outcomes; and on the other, it means that there will be a variety of public funds, holding companies or banks undertaking investment in competition with one another within a shared framework of legislation. Thus a broad social equality will be achieved partly by suppressing large-scale private property but also by income supplements and taxation. The general aim would be to secure the allocative advantages of the market with respect to investment while removing its distributional injustice with respect to income.[12]

Traditional socialists always pointed to the fact that market models could hardly guarantee social justice, not to mention equality. But from the point of view of their opponents:

> even should community and self-esteem be compromised by competition, the market-socialist proposals, if enacted, would still mark progress toward a just society. The improvement in the distribution of wealth and income and the reduction of public bads that they would bring, if the theory is correct, would greatly increase the opportunities for self-realization and welfare of those who would have been much worse off under capitalism.[13]

The problem with capitalism, however, is not only in distribution, it is also in the way it allocates resources and structures investment. While socialists now are discovering the relative advantages of the market, capitalism itself is evolving in a completely different direction. Multinational corporations, which dominate the global economy, really do compete between themselves, but this competition has very little to do with the traditional market behaviour as described in the books of Adam Smith or Karl Marx. The corporations not only do a lot of planning, they even impose their own regulation on the states, influencing government policies in the spheres of taxation, interest rates, social standards and public investment. This regulation is basically anti-social and anti-ecological and it is aimed at subordinating public interests to private profit.

Even the nature of competition changed. In Adam Smith's times competition was undertaken via price cuts of goods and services. But in the times of globalization everything is different. Now nations have to compete for private investment.

As Canadian economist James Rinehart writes:

Competitiveness now means not cheap prices but which workers, which taxpayers, which provinces, and which countries can give the most to the corporation in exchange for new investment or to insure that work does not move elsewhere. While workers compete against each other in a concessions race to the bottom, corporations have found ways of avoiding or cushioning dog-eat-dog competition. Ford owns 25 percent of Mazda and has joint ventures with Volkswagen; General Motors has joint ventures with Toyota, Suzuki and Fiat, Chrysler was allied with Mitsubishi.[14]

At the same time corporations deliberately force their own plants to compete against each other in order to bring labour costs down further. Is this exactly the kind of economic mechanism we want to have in a socialist society?

What we see now in globalized capitalism is an interaction of some remaining market mechanisms with competitive private planning. The real problem is not in socializing the markets (they are increasingly being socialized by capitalism itself) but in socializing and democratizing the planning, in replacing private strategic decision-making by public policies. That also means going beyond the profit motive as the basic incentive for economic activities and changing the criteria according to which we judge enterprise performance.

The neo-liberal culture of the 1990s created a real cult of modern management capable of achieving best performance through inventiveness, competence and professionalism. The reality was somewhat different but the left, as often happens, swallowed the myth completely uncritically. Though workers' participation in management is still considered desirable, the emphasis is mainly on competence. 'Why could not publicly owned banks hire investment specialists or managers just as banks or pension funds do in today's capitalism?', asks Robin Blackburn.[15] And John Roemer is certain that for socialism to work perfectly one just needs to guarantee that management is 'evaluated on economic criteria only'.[16]

This 'pure economic criteria' does not exist in the real world, even in the capitalist corporations. When there are real people there are always personal judgements and individual criteria, which can also be subject to change. Any type of management is based on some collective bureaucratic or corporatist ethics. If you fit into a particular pattern, your performance is going to be judged more favourably. Managers (as well as academics) base their career on reputation. And this reputation depends, last but not least, on the ability of the managers to serve the interests of the capital.

Socialists must not base their approach on repeating such nonsense about 'pure economic criteria' for management. On the contrary, the left has to develop its own performance criteria and managerial ethics for public sector. Instead of internalizing the visions of the owners, management must be capable of reacting to democratic pressures. It must not care only about profits but find ways to solve the multiple problems of communities, consider the ecological consequences of decisions made and cooperate with colleagues from other public enterprises.

Ironically, market socialists became intellectual hostages of the liberal ideologues whom they criticize so strongly. Their idealization of the market is based on the assumption that the world will always remain the same as it is now. In reality, the world always changed and will keep changing. Even within capitalism the role and the very form of the market was different in different historic periods. For that reason, market mechanisms cannot be simply rejected by the left: in a different social and institutional context they will also change. But at the same time we must remember that the historic meaning of socialism for Marx was to overcome the dependency of people on 'blind' uncontrollable economic forces. Actually, in modern capitalism these forces are not completely uncontrollable. They are just controlled by the few, against the interests of the many. The failures of modern capitalism do not come from a lack of control over the economic system but from the nature of this control. Being undemocratic, this control can't be efficient. Bureaucratic struggles inside corporations are no less important for decision-making than the structure of prices and marketing strategies. In a situation when huge power is concentrated in a completely undemocratic manner, short-term private gain inevitably becomes prioritized over the sustainability of the system. The negative consequences of decisions made by 'competent management' are ignored even when they are evident. This creates the impression that the anarchy of spontaneous economic forces typical of the earlier stages of capitalism re-emerges at the level of the globalized economy. In reality, it is the anarchy of bureaucratic corporate decision-making, which has at least as much to do with hyper-centralization as with the blind forces of the market.

The Socialist alternative is needed precisely because non-market allocation of resources is now necessary and unavoidable. The difference between current corporate investment and the socialized investment is that the public sector must be transparent, accountable, democratic, with decisions open to debate. It must prioritize ecological, social and humane development over profits. And development also must be sustainable, which is not possible in conditions where private interests dominate.

It is very characteristic that today's market-socialists concentrate their efforts on describing increasingly abstract models instead of discussing concrete proposals of economic transformation. At the same time, traditional socialists spend most time criticizing their pro-market colleagues without offering a clear alternative. That is absolutely inevitable in a period when socialist practice is poor. That is why many questions are not formulated correctly. For example, socialist transformation can only be started in the context of capitalist historic past and thus inevitably any feasible socialism at the first stage is doomed to be a kind of 'market socialism'. A mixed economy is the best strategy to navigate out of capitalism. But this doesn't mean that the market is an ideal mechanism for socialist economics. On the contrary, during the development of a new society and economy we can overcome the limitations of the market, and that is exactly why socialism is historically necessary. In the long run all these problems will not be resolved through theoretical debates. The only way forward to find answers is through practice.

Ironically, today the best answer to theoretical problems is political radicalism. As a result of the collapse of the Soviet system and the globalization of capitalism, left-reformist politics, at least as they have been understood to date, have in practice become impossible. The social and political space for reforms has become extremely narrow. This does not mean that reforms within the framework of capitalism are becoming impossible in principle, but the preconditions for such changes are having to be created afresh. It is necessary, so to speak, to break open society's political space. In the 1980s it was still possible to speak of revolutionary reforms, while placing the stress on the word 'reforms'. But as the new century approaches, the stress must be on the revolutionary aspects. The important thing is not how radical the new reformist project will be, but that the project will be impossible in principle unless there are new revolutionary upheavals.

One has to agree with Canadian Marxist Darko Suvin:

> we have no choice but to propose the most daring utopia, which is today, to begin with, not Earthly Paradise but the prevention of Hell on Earth. May the Earth remain our habitable mother rather than being pushed by greedy class and imbecilitated masses (as today) the way of ecological catastrophe, and the ensuing great Migration of Peoples, the bitter State and corporation wars, the civil wars of constructed racism and ethnicity! But paradoxically, I am persuaded that *finally* – which is not at all opposed to other medium-range horizons – only the most radical counterpoise, a flexible system of what Marx called the free association of direct producers, the horizon of a global self-sustaining and self-managing society – which is socialism –, has a chance: only by mobilizing Paradise or Utopia, can Hell or Fascism be defeated.[17]

However, radical utopias make sense only when they cease to be utopian and when social criticism becomes part of the struggle to reconstruct the society. That was the original message of Marxist socialism and it is as important now as it was in the days of Marx. Maybe even more.

The present epoch understandably evokes comparisons both with the later centuries of the Roman Empire, and also with the period of the early bourgeois revolutions. The Eurocentric world has twice passed through historical transitions, when one type of society has been replaced by another. Today we are embarking on a third such passage. In the past these processes have taken centuries, and we should not assume that history now works more rapidly. However the means of communication might have changed, human psychology and the behaviour of large groups of people remain subject to their own laws and rhythms. The effect of the new technologies has not been to make the processes quicker, but to make them more global. The collapse of ancient society took place on the scale of the Mediterranean Sea. The rise of capitalism occurred on the scale of the European-Atlantic world, including in its orbit India and parts of Africa. Now the Eurocentric world has become identical to the geographical world.

The transition from antiquity to feudalism was accompanied by the decline of civilization and by the lengthy epoch of the 'dark ages'. It took many centuries before European society acquired the potential for new growth and, after regaining its former level, began developing at an accelerated pace. The epoch of the crisis of feudalism and of the rise of capitalism was a time of social convulsions, many of them bloody. But it also saw impressive cultural achievements and economic growth. What will the third transition be like? Ultimately, this depends on us.

We are responsible for the future and we simply have to act according to our principles. Like Shakespeare's Hamlet we have to stop our endless hesitation and say: 'The readiness is all.'

Notes

Preface

1. J.O. Andersson. 'Fundamental Values for a Third Left'. *New Left Review*, March–April 1996, no. 216.
2. S. Amin. *Re-Reading the Post-War Period: An Intellectual Itinerary*. New York, 1994.

Introduction: Pride and Protest

1. *After the Fall: The Failure of Communism and the Future of Socialism*. Ed. by R. Blackburn. London and New York, 1992, p. 239.
2. See *The New Times: The Changing Face of Politics in the 1990s*. Ed. by S. Hall and M. Jacques. London and New York, 1990, pp. 335, 411, 378.

1 Does Trade Unionism Have a Future?

1. *USA Today*/International edition, 14 June 1995.
2. *Die Mitbestimmung*. Spetsial'nyy vypusk zhurnala Fonda im. Kh. Beklera na russkom yazyke, 1995, p. 51.
3. *USA Today*/International edition, 14 June 1995.
4. M. Castells. *The Information Age*. Malden and Oxford, 1998, vol. I, p. 277.
5. *Korea Times*, 25 April 1996, p. 3.
6. *Labor Power* (international bulletin of the Philippine labour movement), July 1996, vol. I, no. 1, p. 5.
7. R. Harbridge and A. Honeybone. 'External Legitimacy of the Unions: Trends in New Zealand.' Paper presented to the Second International Conference on Emerging Union Structures, Stockholm, 11–14 June 1995, p. 12. Hereafter: Stockholm Conference Paper. See also *The Future of Trade Unionism: International Perspectives on Emerging Union Structures*. Ed. by M. Sverke. Aldershot, UK, 1997.
8. *Le Monde Diplomatique*, July 1996, p. 7.
9. See *Voprosy ekonomiki*, 1995, no. 6, p. 108.
10. Ibid., p. 106.
11. *Labour Focus on Eastern Europe*, 1998, no. 60, p. 52.

161

12.   *Voprosy ekonomiki*, 1995 no. 6, p. 108. The development of Russian trade unions did not confirm the expectations of many leftists who predicted the growth of militancy and successful reform of union bureaucracy. However, it did not confirm the predictions of some radical critics of union bureaucracy who saw official unions 'on the road to a shameful death' (*Russian Labour Review*, 1993, no. 1, p. 14). On unionism in Eastern Europe in the mid-1990s see also *Labour Focus on Eastern Europe*, 1996, no. 55 (a special issue on trade unions).

13.   *Moscow Times*, 17 February 1999.

14.   *Korea Times*, 25 April 1996, p. 2.

15.   See L. Lindstrom. *Accumulation, Regulation, and Political Struggles: Manufacturing Workers in South Korea*. University of Stockholm, Studies in Politics 46, 1993, pp. 122, 126, 172.

16.   *Korea Focus*, March–April 1998, vol. 6, no. 2, p. 51.

17.   *Korea Times*, 25 April 1996, p. 3.

18.   *Le Monde Diplomatique*, February 1997, no. 515, p. 19. Liberal commentators also agree that 'in all the major Asian economies today labor is assuming a critical new importance. For one thing, with millions of manufacturing jobs added in the region since 1985, industrial workers have become a more powerful force. At the same time, labor's key demands for higher wages and a better life are exactly the medicine that Asia's sick tigers need to regain their economic health' (*Moscow Times*, 3 March 1998).

19.   *Monthly Review*, September 1998, vol. 50, no. 4, p. 13.

20.   A. Callinicos. *South Africa between Reform and Revolution*. London, 1988, p. 102. Johann Maree. 'The Changing Role and Perception of Members as Unions Grow.' Stockholm Conference Paper, p. 9.

21.   I. Macun. 'Growth, Structure and Power in the South African Union Movement.' Stockholm Conference Paper.

22.   K. von Holdt. 'From Politics of Resistance to Politics of Reconstruction? The Union and "Ungovernability" in the Workplace.' Stockholm Conference Paper, p. 21.

23.   Ibid.

24.   A. Callinicos, *South Africa*, pp. 5, 7.

25.   *South African Labour Bulletin*, July 1994, vol. 18, no. 3, p. 25.

26.   Ibid., p. 10.

27.   E.O. Akwetey. *Trade Unions and Democratisation: A Comparative Study of Zambia and Ghana*. University of Stockholm, Studies in Politics 50, 1994, p. 109.

28.   *South African Labour Bulletin*, March 1995, vol. 19, no. 1, p. 85.

29.   *South African Labour Bulletin*, May 1994, vol. 18, no. 2, p. 52.

30.   *South African Labour Bulletin*, July 1994, vol. 18, no. 3, p. 88.

31. See E. Sader and K. Silverstein. *Without Fear of Being Happy: Lula and the Workers' Party in Brazil*. London, 1991, p. 39.
32. *Green Left Weekly*, 4 June 1997, p. 18.
33. *Rising From the Ashes? Labor in the Age of 'Global' Capitalism*. Ed. by E. Meiksins Wood, P. Meiksins and M. Yates. New York, 1998, p. 149.
34. *Far Eastern Economic Review*, 16 May 1996.
35. *Labor Power*, July 1996, vol. 1, no. 1, p. 5.
36. D. Sassoon, *One Hundred Years of Socialism*. London and New York, 1996, pp. 34, 653–55.
37. W. Hutton, *The State We're In*. London, 1996, p. 85.
38. *Socialist Register 1996*. Ed. by L. Panitch. New York and Halifax, 1996, p. 153.
39. *Rouge*, 6 December 1995.
40. Ibid.
41. *Le Monde*, 7 December 1995.
42. D. Singer. *Whose Millennium? Theirs or Ours?* New York, 1999, p. 4.
43. *Links*, July–November 1996, no. 7, p. 72.
44. D. Sassoon, *One Hundred Years of Socialism*, p. 357.
45. *OCAW Reporter*, July–August 1996, vol. 52, no. 5–6, p. 4.
46. D. Singer, *Whose Millennium?*, p. 209.
47. For an account of the processes occurring in the Italian trade unions, see P. Di Nicola. 'Formal and Informal Representativeness in Italy: Members and Voters of the Confederal Trade Unions.' Stockholm Conference Paper.
48. *Analises et documents économiques*, December 1994, no. 62. *Cahiers du centre confédéral d'études économiques et sociales de la CGT*. Dossier: Vues sur l'économie française: reprise conjoncturelle et enjeux structurels, p. 7.
49. Ibid., p. 77.
50. *Monthly Review*, July–August 1996, vol. 48, no. 3, pp. 17–18.
51. E. Meiksins et al., *Rising From the Ashes?*, p. 36. See also Anna Pollert in *Socialist Register 1996*. London, 1996, p. 159.
52. W. Higgins. 'The Swedish Municipal Workers Union: A Study in the New Political Unionism.' Stockholm Conference Paper.
53. A. Pape. 'Trade Union Structure and Institutional Framework for Labour Relations: Organisational Reforms in the Norwegian Confederations of Trade Unions'; T. Andersen. 'Decentralisation of Pay Bargaining in the Danish Public Sector: Local Strategies of Conflict Handling'. Stockholm Conference Paper.
54. *Alfaguara*, November 1996, no. 16, pp. 27, 28.
55. *Critique Communiste*, Winter 1996–97, no. 147, p. 47.
56. Kim Moody, American labour movement theorist, calls that 'social movement unionism' which will inevitably prefigure 'a deeper socialist politics' (K. Moody. *Workers in a Lean World*.

London and New York, 1997, p. 309). See also S. Cohen and K. Moody. 'Unions, Strikes and Class Consciousness Today.' *Socialist Register 1998*. London and New York, 1998.

2 Beyond Identities

1. S. Ewen. *All Consuming Images*. New York, 1988, p. 112.
2. *Socialist Review* (SF), 1995, vol. 25, no. 3–4, p. 10.
3. *Nezavisimaya Gazeta*, 22 June 1996, p. 7.
4. A. Giddens. *Beyond Left and Right: The Future of Radical Politics*. Cambridge, 1994, p. 113. Another fashionable author who tells us stories about going beyond left and right and the perspectives of radical democracy is Roberto Mangabiera Unger. According to him the old contest between statism and privatism, command and market, is dying. It is replaced by a more promising rivalry among alternative institutional forms of economic, social and political pluralism. The basic promise of this new conflict is that market economies, free civil societies and representative democracies can assume different institutional forms, with rather different consequences for society. (Roberto Mangabiera Unger. *The Progressive Alternative*. London and New York, 1998, p. 3). Social conflict is hardly mentioned; it looks as if we are already in a classless society. Instead of the struggle for social change we are offered a prospect of democratic experimentation within the capitalist system. The problem is that this experimentalism without social confrontation and without the old conflict between public and private makes very little sense for anyone outside the neo-liberal political establishment. It is not clear, however, why Unger's book is called *The Progressive Alternative*. *Reactionary Self-Praise* would be more accurate.
5. A. Giddens, *Beyond Left and Right*, p. 14.
6. Ibid., p. 196.
7. Ibid., p. 197.
8. *Commodify your Dissent*. Ed. by T. Frank and M. Weiland. New York and London, 1997, pp. 34–5. The same in: *The Baffler*, 1995, no. 6, p. 15.
9. Ibid. See also T. Frank. *The Conquest of Cool*. Chicago and London, 1997.
10. *Encyclopedia of the American Left*. Ed. by M.J. Buhle, P. Buhle and D. Georgakas. New York and London, 1990, p. xii.
11. F. Jameson. *Postmodernism, or The Cultural Logic of Late Capitalism*. Durham, NC, 1992, p. 48. See also F. Jameson. 'Actually Existing Marxism'. In: *Beyond Marxism*. Ed. by S. Maksidi, C. Casarino and R.E. Karl. New York, 1996; F. Jameson. *Seeds of Time*. New York, 1994.

12. *Socialist Review* (SF), 1995, vol. 25, nos 3–4, p. 4.
13. Ibid., p. 67.
14. Ibid., p. 80.
15. *Links*, July–October 1996, no. 7, p. 22.
16. *Sovremennaya zapadnaya sotsiologiya*. Ed. by Per Manson. St Petersburg, 1992, p. 230.
17. *Nezavisimaya Gazeta*, 17 March 1993.
18. *Feminism: The Essential Historical Writings*. Ed. by M. Schneir. New York, 1972.
19. *PDS Pressedienst*, 1996, no. 47, p. 10.
20. D. Sassoon, *One Hundred Years of Socialism*. pp. 392–3.
21. *Feminism and Socialism*. Chippendale, Australia, 1992, p. 8.
22. *Nezavisimaya Gazeta*, 17 March, 1993.
23. S. Rowbotham, L. Segal and H. Wainwright. *Beyond the Fragments*. London, 1979.
24. D. Sassoon, *One Hundred Years of Socialism*, p. 440.
25. Ibid., p. 688.
26. Ibid., p. 675. It was shocking for feminists of the 1990s to discover that Nazi Germany also had been one of the countries with relatively good perspectives of social mobility for women. See *Feminismes et nazisme*. Ed. by Lilianne Kandel. Paris, 1997.
27. N. Bobbio, *Left and Right: The Significance of a Political Distinction*, Cambridge, 1996, p. 11.
28. *Feminism and Socialism*, p. 34. Academic studies show that in many countries parties of the right promote women to top positions almost as often as parties of the left.

    Although it has been frequently suggested that parties of the left tend to be more favorably disposed than those of the right to sharing leadership with women, scholars are not unanimous on this point. . . . Further, recent work cites evidence from Scandinavia, Canada, and West Germany that parties of the right are no less willing than parties of the left to nominate and elect women. (R.H. Davis. *Women and Power in Parliamentary Democracies*. Lincoln and London, 1997, pp. 57–8).

29. D. Sassoon, *One Hundred Years of Socialism*, p. 674.
30. *Feminism and Socialism*, p. 35.
31. *Nezavisimaya Gazeta*, 17 March 1993.
32. R. Denfeld. *The New Victorians*. New York, 1995. There is a striking continuity between American feminism and Protestant values (in both cases there is a deep suspicion of sexuality, beauty, humour and any kind of *joie de vivre*). This neo-puritanism arouses astonishment and irony in the countries of Eastern Europe. The Moscow journal *Stolitsa* urges its readers to play 'Russian harassment', only not 'for money',

like the Americans, but 'as a diversion, for slaps on the head and for green Gosser beer coasters'. At the same time, the journal remarks that the 'game of harassment' is very helpful to management for maintaining order 'in a healthy capitalist workplace' (*Stolitsa*, 10 March 1997, p. 84). For amusement's sake, readers are offered a separate poster with a full list, drawn up on the basis of American laws and regulations, of the actions falling into the category of harassment. The editors recommended that the poster be pinned up in the workplace, in order to raise the spirits of workers.

33. *Socialist Register 1993*. Ed. by R. Miliband and L. Panitch. London, 1993, p. 100.
34. *Green Left Weekly*, 30 April 1997, p. 23.
35. *Frieden fur Kurdistan – Demokratie fur die Turkei*. Munich, INTERFOBI, 1996, p. 167.
36. *Inprecor*, March 1996, no. 400, p. 15.
37. *Green Left Weekly*, 30 April 1997, p. 23.
38. R. Miliband. *Socialism for a Sceptical Age*. Cambridge, 1994, p. 129.
39. See *Vtoroy s'ezd RSDRP. Protokoly*. Moscow, 1959, pp. 320 and elsewhere.
40. E. Balibar and I. Wallerstein. *Race, Nation, Class*. London and New York, 1991, p. 83.
41. Ibid., p. 84.
42. In this connection, the position of the management of the South Korean company Samsung is very significant. In the words of its executives, the company in the 1990s 'has continued to widen opportunities for women in specialized fields'. This policy has been closely linked with new methods of control over the labour force and with an increase in labour 'flexibility'. According to the Samsung business group, 'companies that fail to fully utilize their female employees will not survive unlimited competition' (*Korea Focus*, March–April 1997, vol. 5, no. 2, p. 93). It is clear that such 'utilization' of female workers has little in common with emancipation.
43. For the corresponding sociological data, see D. Sassoon, *One Hundred Years of Socialism*, pp. 660, 865.
44. A. Brie, *Betreing der Visionen. Fuer eine sozialistiche Erneuerung*. Konkret Literatur Verlag, Hamburg, 1992, p. 126.
45. N. Bukharin. *Tyuremnye rukopisi*. Ed. G.A. Bordyugov and S. Cohen. Moscow, 1996, vol. 1, p. 126.
46. Ibid., pp. 133, 126.
47. M. Marable. *Race, Identity and Political Culture*. Cited in: *Socialist Review* (SF), 1995, no. 2, p. 48.
48. *Socialist Review* (SF), 1995, vol. 25, nos 3–4, p. 7.
49. *Third World Viewpoint*, winter 1996, vol. 1, no. 5, p. 9.

50. *Left Business Observer*, December 1996, no. 75, p. 8. Even among the American left not everyone is excited with politically correct language (PC). Political correctness, we read in an anarchist pamphlet:

> has a very negative effect upon the struggles for racial equality, peace and environmental sanity. The extremism and authoritarianism of the politically correct becomes a brush with which to tar legitimate dissent. . . . Political correctness, by halting debate, or at least confining it within the narrowest of frameworks, is thus destructive of what should be a natural evolution of critical political and social thought. (L. Gambone. *Laughter is Bourgeois!* New York, 1995, p. 9).

51. C. Mouffe. *The Return of the Political.* London, 1988, pp. 19, 18.
52. See E. Laclau and C. Mouffe. *Hegemony and Socialist Strategy: Towards a Radical Democratic Politics.* London and New York, 1985; E. Laclau. *New Reflections on the Revolution of Our Time.* London and New York, 1990; C. Mouffe. *The Return of the Political.*
53. C. Mouffe. *The Return of the Political,* p. 100. Not all the supporters of postmodern politics see universalism as something to be rejected. For example Göran Therborn, one of the co-authors of a famous book *The New Times* sees in his views 'a basic continuity with modern socialism, in universalism, in historicity, and in concentrating on scrutinising and changing the content of social and political forms' (*The New Times: The Changing Face of Politics in the 1990s.* Ed. by S. Hall and M. Jacques. London and New York, 1990, p. 438). It is very telling that this kind of continuity connects the authors of *New Times* with liberalism as much as with socialism. There is nothing specifically leftist in accepting the possibility of change in social and political forms. It is the content of this change which is essential. It is also very telling that, according to Therborn, the connection between socialism and life politics is historical, it is based on 'a sense of link' (p. 439). It is more personal than political. This link becomes necessary because postmodernist intellectuals do not dare to reject their leftist and Marxist past completely but at the same time they do not want to accept any socialist or leftist commitments for the future. However the logic of postmodern dictates the need to reject not just socialist commitments but also universalism and, finally, the very principle of democracy which is based on universalism as well.
54. *New Politics*, Winter 1997, vol. 6, no. 2, pp. 58, 59.
55. C. Lasch. *The Revolt of the Elites and the Betrayal of Democracy.* New York and London, 1996, p. 91.

56. T. Ebert. *Ludic Feminism and After.* Ann Arbor, 1996, p. 3.
57. *Monthly Review,* July–August 1996, vol. 48, no. 3, pp. 30, 32.
58. T. Gitlin. *The Twilight of Common Dreams: Why America is Wracked by Culture Wars.* New York, 1995, pp. 215, 216. Slavoj Zizek has also written on 'leftist enlightenment' as an alternative to 'elitist multicultural liberalism' (*New Left Review,* September–October 1997, no. 225, pp. 47, 51).
59. *New Politics,* winter 1997, vol. 6, no. 2, p. 86.
60. *Socialist Review* (SF), 1995, no. 2, p. 68.
61. E. Meiksins Wood. *The Retreat from Class.* London and New York, 1986, p. 153.
62. *Green Left Weekly,* 24 July 1996, p. 22.
63. A. Sivanandan. *Communities of Resistance: Writings on Black Struggles for Socialism.* London and New York, 1990, p. 85. On Afrocentrist ideologies as a mirror image of bourgeois Eurocentrism see S. Howe. *Afrocentrism: Mythical Pasts and Imagined Homes.* London, 1998.
64. *After the Fall: The Failure of Communism and the Future of Socialism.* Ed. by R. Blackburn. London and New York, 1992, p. 283.
65. *Nezavisimaya Gazeta,* 23 January 1997, p. 6.
66. *Nezavisimaya Gazeta,* 11 April 1996.
67. *Links,* July–October 1996, no. 7, p. 19.
68. Ibid., p. 22.
69. A. Sivanandan, *Communities of Resistance,* pp. 84–5.
70. *New Politics,* 1996, vol. 5, no. 4, p. 80.
71. Ibid., p. 79.
72. Iris Young. 'Unruly Categories: A Critique of Nancy Foster's Dual Systems Theory'. *New Left Review,* March–April 1997, no. 222, pp. 148, 156.
73. *Green Left Weekly,* 5 February 1997, p. 11.
74. W. Hutton, *The State We're In,* p. 287.
75. *La Nouvelle Alternative,* June 1995, no. 38, p. 11.
76. *Civil Society and the State: New European Perspectives.* Ed. by J. Keane. London and New York, 1988, p. 251.
77. Ibid., p. 254.
78. See, for example, D. Singer. 'The Real Eurobattle'. *The Nation,* 23 December 1996, p. 22; A. Giddens, *Beyond Left and Right,* p. 81.
79. *Nezavisimaya Gazeta. NG-Stsenarii,* 19 September 1996.
80. In the case of Bosnia, this is shown particularly well by the following article: Jens Stilhoff Sorensen. 'Pluralism or Fragmentation?' *War Report,* May 1997, no. 51, pp. 32–3.
81. Some writers, while recognizing the crisis of the new social movements, go so far as to argue that this crisis represents the movements' strong point. Thus André Gunder Frank and Marta Fuentes write that:

the very life-cycle of social movements, which either fade away or become institutionalized, is less a mark of their weakness, irrelevance or self-negation, than it is the living expression of their vitality for and growing importance in the social transformation(s) of the future. (S. Amin, G. Arrighi, A. Gunder Frank and I. Wallerstein. *Transforming the Revolution: Social Movements and the World-System*. New York, 1990, p. 179)

This may be quite sufficient consolation for theoreticians, but for people whose hopes have been deceived by the mirage of the new social movements, it does not sound very convincing. The crisis of these movements does not stem from the fulfilment of their programmes (as is the case with 'classical' liberalism or social democracy, whose programmes have been at least partly fulfilled), but from the fact that they cannot deliver.

82. O. Yanitsky. *Russian Environmentalism: Leading Figures, Facts, Opinions*. Moscow, 1993, p. 7.
83. O. Yanitsky. *Ekologicheskoe dvizhenie v Rossii*. Moscow, 1996, p. 199.
84. *Society and Natural Resources*, 1996, no. 9, p. 75.
85. Quoted in *Green Left Weekly*, 9 July 1999, p. 16.
86. Eric Hobsbawm. 'Identity Politics and the Left'. *New Left Review*, May–June 1996, no. 217, p. 41.
87. T. Gitlin, *The Twilight of Common Dreams*, p. 82.
88. Ibid., p. 95.
89. Ibid., p. 101.
90. Meanwhile, the notion of the 'extra-class' nature of environmental demands has penetrated not only into the documents of 'greens', but also into socialist literature. See, for example, the well-known letter of the brothers Brie, published in *PDS Pressedienst*, 1995, no. 28.
91. *New Politics*, winter 1997, vol. 6, no. 2, p. 97.
92. Ibid., p. 87.
93. Young, 'Unruly Categories', p. 160.
94. *Socialist Register 1998*. London, 1998, pp. 22–3.

3 The Third Left or the Third Socialism

1. J.O. Andersson. 'Fundamental Values for a Third Left.' *New Left Review*, March–April 1996, no. 216, p. 67.
2. Ibid., p. 69.
3. *Utopias*, 1996, vol. 4, no. 170, p. 129.
4. Otto Bauer wrote in 1936:

   The democratic socialism of the West is the heir of the struggle for spiritual and political freedom. The revolutionary socialism of the East is the heir of a revolution aimed at economic and social liberation. It is necessary to unite what development has divided. (O. Bauer. *Zwischen zwei Weltkreisen*. Bratislava, 1936, p. 213)

Bauer named this 'integral socialism'. It is obvious that on the whole the idea of the 'third left' repeats this concept. On Austro-Marxist political concept see Ch. Butterwegge. *Austromarxismus und Staat*. Marburg, 1991.

5. S. Amin. *Re-Reading the Postwar Period: An Intellectual Itinerary*. New York, 1994, p. 192. Speaking in Stockholm in 1995 at a seminar of Marxist theoreticians organized by the Left Party of Sweden, Amin met with criticism from some participants who argued that, despite real changes in the world, substantial possibilities remained for serious struggles at the national level. The thesis of 'globalization' could be used as a justification for opportunism and inertia.

6. Ibid., p. 193.

7. There is evidently some kind of intellectual symbolism in the figure three, forcing people to link with a third phase such concepts as 'maturity', 'revival', 'consolidation', 'synthesis' and so forth. At the same time as Amin spoke of a 'third socialism', and Andersson of a 'third left', the Cuban sociologist Maria I. Rauber wrote of 'the third generation of revolutionaries' coming into being in Latin America. (M.I. Rauber, *Izquierda Latinoamericana: Crisis y Cambio*. Havana, 1993, p. 99). If the first generation was the 'traditional left', inspired by the ideas of the Russian revolution, and the second generation comprised the 'new left', the heirs of the Cuban revolution and the activists of the Chilean and Sandinista revolutions, the third generation is defined using rather diffuse and general references to 'all those who struggle to achieve independence and national development without abandoning the banners of social justice and ethnic equality' (p. 163). In other words, these people for the present are revolutionaries without a revolution. It should be noted that Rauber's book was written before the Zapatista uprising.

8. *Links*, October–December 1994, no. 3.

9. *Green Left Weekly*, 4 October 1995, p. 21.

10. *Shadows of Tender Fury: The Letters and Communiques of Subcomandante Marcos and the Zapatista Army of National Liberation*. New York, 1995, pp. 92–3.

11. Ibid., p. 85.

12. Ibid., p. 29.

13. Ibid., p. 45.

14. *Latinskaya Amerika*, 1996, no. 2, p. 50.

15. *Green Left Weekly*, 4 September 1996, p. 21.

16. *Utopie Critique*, 1997, no. 9, p. 65.
17. *Viento del Sur*, winter 1996, no. 8, p. 35.
18. Ibid., p. 12.
19. *New Left Review*, July–August 1996, no. 218, p. 129.
20. *Utopie Critique*, 1997, no. 9, p. 67.
21. *Viento del Sur*, winter 1996, no. 8, p. 24.
22. For example the insurgent army in southern Sudan declares that it does not intend to storm the capital, but that it is trying 'to use its military victories to provoke a revolution in the north' (*Green Left Weekly*, 12 February 1997, p. 14).
23. Marcos stresses that it was the practical experience of struggle that forced him to change his views. See *Critique communiste*, Winter 1996–97, no. 147, p. 9.
24. *Le Monde Diplomatique*, January 1997, p. 13.
25. See *Estrategia Internacional*, junio/agosto 1999, Buenos Aires, p. 4.
26. *Itogi*, 14 January 1997, nos 1–2, p. 33.
27. Ibid.
28. See *Segodnya*, 22 June 1995; *Moskovskiy Komsomolets*, 30 June 1995, and elsewhere. For a more detailed analysis of the actions of Basayev during the Budennovsk hostage crisis see the following articles: B. Kagarlitsky. 'Chto s nami proiskhodit ili uroki Basaeva'. *Svobodnaya mysl'*, 1995, no. 8; B. Kagarlitsky. 'Chechenskaya voyna i obshchestvennoe mnenie'. *Svobodnaya mysl'*, 1997, no. 1.
29. *Green Left Weekly*, 7 May 1997.
30. *Le Monde Diplomatique*, January 1997, p. 13.
31. *Inprecor*, February 1997, no. 410, p. 34.
32. *Pagina 12* (Buenos Aires), 5 January 1997.
33. *Le Monde Diplomatique*, January 1997, p. 13.
34. *New Left Review*, July–August 1996, no. 218, p. 129.
35. *Rouge*, 19 December 1996; *Green Left Weekly*, 12 February 1997, p. 15.
36. *Moskovskie Novosti*, 1996, no. 47, p. 8.
37. *Itogi*, 1996, no. 18, p. 16.
38. *Green Left Weekly*, 28 May 1997, p. 18.
39. Cited in D. Renzi and M. Zanichelli. *PCI/PDS: Tra crisi e trasformazione*. Roma, 1991, p. 93.
40. L. Bisky, J. Czerny, H. Mayer and M. Schumann (eds). *Die PDS – Herkunft und Selbstverstaendnis*. Berlin, 1996, p. 157.
41. *Von den Anfängen. Eine illustrierte Chronik der PDS, 1989 bis 1994*. Berlin, 1995, S. 11.
42. *Sklaven*, 1997, no. 32–3, pp. 8, 11.
43. *Disput*, 1997, no. 1, p. 11; *PDS Pressedienst*, 18 April 1997, no. 16, p. 3.
44. *PDS Auslandsbulletin*, September 1996, p. 2.
45. Cited in *Al'ternativy*, 1996, no. 1, pp. 99–100.

46. See R. Liebisch. 'Transformierter Ossi noch nicht in Sicht'. *Neues Deutschland*, 1–2 March 1997, p. 20.
47. *Neues Deutschland*, 15–16 February 1997, p. 10.
48. *Ostdeutschland – Herausforderung und Chance.* Parteivorstand der PDS und Bundestagsgruppe PDS, 2 October 1996. Berlin and Bonn, 1996, p. 4.
49. *PDS Auslandsbulletin*, September 1996, p. 2.
50. See *Neues Deutschland*, 4 March 1997. Several surveys gave the PDS 2 per cent of the potential voters in the west. In municipal elections in Kassel and Frankfurt-am-Main the PDS, without any chance of winning, received 1.4–1.6 per cent of the votes.
51. *PDS Pressedienst*, 18 April 1997, no. 16, p. 3.
52. *Linke (wieder) im Bundestag: Opposition konkret.* Bonn, 1994, p. 25.
53. *Inprecor*, March 1996, no. 400, p. 26.
54. *Magdeburg: Modell oder Experiment? Landtags Report Sachsen-Anhalt.* Fraktion der PDS. Magdeburg, 1996, p. 55.
55. Ibid., pp. 71–2. It is worth noting that Lenin considered a rejection of real opportunities for reform to be a political mistake:

    > We always maintain that a socialist party that does not combine this struggle for reforms with the revolutionary methods of the workers' movement is liable to turn into a sect and become divorced from the masses, and that this represents an extremely serious threat to the success of genuine revolutionary socialism. (V.I. Lenin. *Polnoe Sobranie Sochineniy*, Moscow, vol. 27, p. 72).

56. *KPD-Verbot oder mit Kommunisten leben? Opposition konkret.* Hrsg. von Parteivorstand der PDS. Berlin and Bonn, 1996, p. 107.
57. Ibid., p. 109.
58. R. Luxemburg. *Gesammelte Werke.* East Berlin, 1970–75, vol. 1/2, p. 373.
59. *Utopie-Kreativ*, March 1997, no. 77, p. 7.
60. *Disput*, 1997, no. 1, pp. 14, 10.
61. *Labour Focus on Eastern Europe*, 1999, no. 63, p. 94.
62. *PDS Pressedienst*, 1999, no. 27, p. 5.
63. E. Sader and K. Silverstein, *Without Fear of Being Happy: Lula and the Workers' Party in Brazil.* London, 1991, p. 9.
64. Analogous processes have occurred in other Latin American left parties. In the view of James Petras this applies also to *Causa R* in Venezuela, *Frente Amplio* in Uruguay, *Frente Grande* in Argentina and the Revolutionary Democratic Party in Mexico. All these parties and coalitions 'have become sucked into an increasingly electoralist politics and begun to

accommodate to neoliberal policies' ('Latin America: The Resurgence of the Left.' *New Left Review*, May–June 1997, no. 223, p. 22). To the opportunism of the parliamentary parties Petras counterposes the new peasant movements, beginning with the Brazilian Movement of Landless Peasants (MST) and concluding with the Zapatistas. However, these movements are at an early stage of development. Major successes will inevitably lead them to create professional political apparatuses and to commit other 'sins' – otherwise they will be unable to consolidate their gains. The problem, consequently, is not to be solved by counterposing radical 'base' movements to structured parties; the need is to find ways of collaborating, and to open up the political organizations to the demands of spontaneous mass movements. In this respect the Brazilian PT and most of the other 'new wave' parties, despite their shift to the right, differ strikingly both from social democracy and from the communist parties of the past.

65. *Inprecor*, March 1996, no. 400, p. 30.
66. E. Sader. *Governar para todos*. São Paulo, 1992, p. 60.
67. See Raul Pont. 'The Left and Local Government: The Porto Alegre Experience in Brazil.' *Links*, January–April 1996, no. 6.
68. E. Sader, *Government para todos*, p. 122.
69. *Inprecor*, March 1996, no. 407, p. 27.
70. *Labour Focus on Eastern Europe*, 1996, no. 53, p. 75.
71. On Ukrainian electoral statistics see *Correspondances Internationales*, new series, October–December 1998, 15.
72. *Vibir*, 1997, nos 1–2, p. 12.
73. Ibid., p. 108.
74. See V. Kizima. 'Oktiabr', istoria, Ukraina.' *Vibir*, 1997, nos 3–4.
75. For an overview of this debate (from the anti-Lukashenko side) see vol. Masliukov. 'A Report from Minsk'. *Monthly Review*, September 1998, vol. 50, no. 4.
76. On the Russian left during 1993–95 see B. Kagarlitsky. *Restoration in Russia*. London and New York, 1995.
77. *Monthly Review*, October 1995, vol. 47, no. 5, p. 32.
78. G. Gysi (ed.). *Wir brauchen einen dritten Weg*. Hamburg, 1990, p. 57.
79. *Capitalism, Nature, Socialism. A Journal of Socialist Ecology*, June 1993, vol. 4, no. 14, p. 17.
80. *Towards a New Monetary Policy*. Publ. by the Alliance. Wellington, 1998, p. 33.
81. *Internationale linke Parteiprogramme: Eine Documentation*. Hrsg. von Grundsatzkommission beim Parteivorstand der PDS, Berlin, nd, p. 68.
82. *Inprecor*, February 1997, no. 410, p. 31.
83. In Sweden the Left Party achieved much better results. In 1995 it took 12.9 per cent in the European elections, which

was its largest share of the vote ever, but in 1999 it increased its presence in the European parliament receiving 15.5 per cent of the vote. That happened in elections in which the Social Democrats, who traditionally dominated Swedish politics, won only 26.1 per cent. The success of the Left Party cannot be explained by its politics, which are not very different from those of the Socialist Left Party in Norway and the Socialist People's Party of Denmark. The difference, however, is that the Left Party is the only leftist alternative to social democrats available in Sweden. The party, though becoming increasingly moderate, also possesses a visible radical current. On the evolution of Scandinavian left-wing socialist parties see the first book of *Recasting Marxism*: B. Kagarlitsky. *New Realism, New Barbarism*. London, 1999, p. 24. See also *Inprecor*, 1999, no. 437–8.

84. *Green Left Weekly*, 7 July 1999, p. 14.
85. Quoted in *Green Left Weekly*, 23 June 1999, p. 18.
86. *Socialist Campaign Group News*, July 1999, p. 6
87. For an example of a left-wing social democratic theorizing in Germany see Uli Schoeler. *Ein Gespenst verschwand in Europa: Ueber Marx und die sozialistische Idee nach dem Scheitern des sowjetischeb Staatsozialismus*. Bonn, 1999. In many ways, the leftist social democrats of the 1990s are not much different from the mainstream Social Democrats of the 1960s and early 1970s. That tells us to what extent these parties have moved to the right. At the same time, it is possible to say now that, ironically, the left opposition in these parties represents the only 'authentic' social democracy.
88. *Disput*, 1996, no. 10, p. 17.
89. *Disput*, 1996, no. 11, p. 16.
90. E. Sader and K. Silverstein, *Without Fear of Being Happy*, p. 164.
91. See *Green Left Weekly*, 26 March 1997.
92. *Red Pepper*, March 1997, p. 13.
93. *Al'ternativy*, 1996, no. 1, p. 105.
94. *Mainstream*, 14 October 1995, vol. 33, no. 47, p. 3.
95. *PDS Pressedienst*, 1995/1996, no. 52/1, p. 39.
96. *Transitions*, May 1998, p. 55.
97. See G.G. Pirogov. '"Kommunitarizm", kapitalisticheskoe obshchestvo i sotsialisticheskaya mysl'. In: T. Timofeev, R. Yevzerov and B. Kagarlitsky (eds). *Problemy obshchestvennykh preobrazovaniy*. Moscow, 1997, pp. 124–5.
98. *Neues Deutschland*, 3 March 1997.
99. *Pravda*, 18 May 1996.
100. A. Gramsci. *Izbrannye proizvedeniya*, Moscow, vol. 3, p. 174.
101. *El Rodoballo*, 1998–99, no. 9, p. 32.

Conclusion: The Stage We are In

1. A. Buzgalin. *Budushchee kommunizma*. Moscow, 1996, p. 34.
2. V.I. Lenin. *Polnoe sobranie sochineniy*, Moscow, vol. 23, p. 146; vol. 27, p. 62.
3. Ibid., vol. 27, p. 425.
4. A. Buzgalin. *Belaya vorona*. Moscow, 1993, pp. 199–200.
5. *Al'ternativy*, 1995, no. 4, pp. 164, 165.
6. P. Anderson. *A Zone of Engagement*. London, 1992, pp. 336, 341. A collection of articles by French and German left intellectuals, dealing with the lessons of the mass actions by workers in the years from 1995 to 1997, speaks of 'protest without alternatives' (P. Bourdieu, C. Debons, D. Hensche, B. Lutz et al. *Perspektiven des Protests: Initiativen für einem europäischen Wohlfahrtstaat*. Hamburg, 1997, p. 7).
7. It is enough to take a few publications of recent times in order to be convinced that 'after the fall' (to use the terminology of Robin Blackburn) socialist theory has continued to develop. On the 'market socialist' side, see, for example: D. Elson. 'The Economics of a Socialised Market.' In *After the Fall. The Failure of Communism and the Future of Socialism*. Ed. by R. Blackburn. London and New York, 1992; A. Nove. *The Economics of Feasible Socialism Revisited*. London, 1991; R. Miliband. *Socialism for a Sceptical Age*. Cambridge, 1994, etc. For some recent criticisms of 'market socialism' see D. McNally. 'The Impasse of Market Socialism'. *New Politics*, summer 1999, vol. 7, no. 3 (27).
8. Nove, *Feasible Socialism*, p. 263.
9. Blackburn (ed.), *After the Fall*, p. 226.
10. See J.E. Roemer. *A Future for Socialism*. London, 1994, p. 20. For his views on property see J.E. Roemer. *Free to Lose: An Introduction to Marxist Economic Philosophy*. Cambridge, MA, 1988, pp. 148–66. *Analytical Marxism*. Ed. by J.E. Roemer. Cambridge, New York, Paris, 1986, pp. 274–8.
11. G. Dauncey. *After the Crash: The Emergence of the Rainbow Economy*. Basingstoke, 1988, p. 201. On the 'stakeholding' economy see W. Hutton. *The State We're In*. London, 1996, pp. 298–318.
12. Blackburn (ed.), *After the Fall*, p. 223.
13. J.E. Roemer, *A Future for Socialism*, p. 122.
14. *Monthly Review*, October 1995, vol. 47, no. 5, pp. 17, 16.
15. Blackburn (ed.), *After the Fall*, p. 224.
16. J.E. Roemer, *A Future for Socialism*, p. 76.
17. *Utopian Studies*, 1998, vol. 9, no. 2, p. 185.

Index

Compiled by Sue Carlton

176